SIX HISTORIANS

SIX HISTORIANS

By

Ferdinand Schevill

THE UNIVERSITY OF CHICAGO PRESS

ILLUSTRATIONS BY NINA TURNER

Library of Congress Catalog Number: 56-6635

THE UNIVERSITY OF CHICAGO PRESS, CHICAGO 37
Cambridge University Press, London, N.W. 1, England
The University of Toronto Press, Toronto 5, Canada

© *1956 by The University of Chicago. Published 1956. Composed and printed by* THE UNIVERSITY OF CHICAGO PRESS,
Chicago, Illinois, U.S.A.

INTRODUCTION[1]

On my eightieth birthday a group of my University of Chicago friends and colleagues graciously resolved to mark the occasion with a formal dinner. As I had for many years cultivated the habit of wandering beyond the limits of my department in order to enlarge my mental outlook by association with representatives of fields of study other than history, it was an assortment of diverse and yet related minds which gathered for the celebration. Inevitably after a succession of generous toasts had wished on my already bowed head a double and treble portion of my just concluded sum of years, the moment arrived for me to offer to my well-wishers—all like myself troubled with the current agitation over the never settled problems of education and culture—the views I had reached, in this closing period of my life, on the importance of history.

I had made no special preparation for my pronouncement, but, since history had become a very polemical subject in recent decades, I was crammed with definite opinions to which I had attained in the course of the continuing debate and which I poured out with unchecked fervor. I began by

1. Ferdinand Schevill died on December 10, 1954, in Tucson, Arizona, at the age of eighty-six. These incomplete notes, the beginning of an introduction to the essays in this book, were on his desk when he died. To them I have added his two major statements about the writing of history, from the *History of Florence* and *The Great Elector*, which I think will clarify for the reader the main idea in this unfinished introduction: history is literature, not science.

The essays appear as originally written except for some minor editorial changes.—JAMES SCHEVILL.

asserting that history had been practiced in many different manners through the human past and that these differences had yielded a wide variety of uneven and often contradictory results. I went on to say that while a sharp analysis could in all probability reduce these differences to some extent, they could never be wholly removed because of the impossibility of bringing to a common permanent denominator the thinking of successive generations of men immersed in the ever changing tide of time. The facts, let it be noted, with which the historian constructs his picture of the past suffer no change, although continued research may greatly increase their sum. A group of equally endowed historical writers might be concerned to set them forth in essentially identical form. But on their taking the next step, which is to communicate the meaning of the event or events described, the facts will fall violently apart, since each author will endow them with a set of values which are not inherent in the facts but which derive from his particular subjective understanding of life.

[Here the Introduction breaks off and ends with the following notes]:

Illustrate with the changing view of Julius Caesar. The bare facts of his career at everybody's disposal, but the significance of the man and his career has radically opposed evaluations.

The thinking about Julius Caesor is historically more important than the facts, though the facts remain fundamental for any judgment on him.

Augustan Age exalted Caesar. Where did Dante stand? Where Machiavelli and Mommsen?

The case of Hamilton and Jefferson.

Argue for history as a combination of scholarship and philosophy. Conceivably scholarship carried to its greatest refinement may arrive at an unchallengeable body of data. But it is inconceivable that historians should ever arrive at an identical evaluation not subject to fluctuation.

Conclusion—History is literature, not science. Share of skilful writing is a third factor.

FROM THE "INTRODUCTION: ON FLORENTINE HISTORIOGRAPHY"[2]

First legend, then history—that is the inevitable succession among all groups and peoples which, by steadily advancing in the command of themselves and their environment, at last achieve a notable civilization. On reaching the stage at which history definitely rules, they usually give evidence of an increasing self-esteem by somewhat contemptuously affixing to the version of the past, so long the cherished possession of their ancestors, the label "legend" and by dismissing it from consideration as the negligible offspring of ignorance and fancy. At the very least they develop a certain skepticism regarding it, simultaneously welcoming the factual and critical version of their past put forth by the representatives of the new culture. This they affirm to be history, meaning thereby a product which, in distinction from legend handed down by word of mouth and reshaped by each narrator according to his pleasure, is reliable, accurate, and certain because based on the facts as revealed by the surviving records. In short, the position of the later, more enlightened generations is that legend is fiction, history truth, and that whereas men were once content to receive the story of their past from their dreamers and poets, they now take it from their scholars and historians in command of a method

2. Ferdinand Schevill, *History of Florence* (New York: Harcourt, Brace & Co., 1936).

of investigation calculated to yield a full and satisfying knowledge. . . .

Owing to the expansive nature of Western culture and its amazing ability ever to renew itself, the seventeenth and eighteenth centuries, as we have seen, glimpsed fresh possibilities by the use of a more comprehensive and critical method than the one employed by the historians of Greece and Rome. These pioneering centuries uncovered the value of original documents and in the course of their long-continued occupation with them gradually shaped the numerous techniques which in their sum constitute our vaunted modern scholarship.

But let us make no mistake: scholarship is a portal, not a goal. It deals with the records left behind by the past, not as though they were an end in themselves, but in order that the unusual and rare scholar who combines creative gifts of mind with the stern discipline of research may set forth a more accurate and authentic version of the past. Hence the modern historian, though he must be refreshed at the well of scholarship and emancipated from the narrow, older methods, is still required, like the classical historians, the original inventors of this form of literature, to prove himself an artist. It is his task to take over the voluminous and sifted data of innumerable scholarly helpers and to give them an order and a meaning, rendering them intelligible and quickening to his generation. Thus both consciously and unconsciously (for much of the labor of every artist is of the unconscious kind), he impresses a particular stamp on his work which is not native to the facts. "It dates" is the current phrase by which we admit the presence in every literary production, including history, of characteristics which do not derive from the material itself but from its treatment by an individual mind. Did we not detect mind behind the legend, behind Villani's candid narrative, behind the writings of both the earlier and the later humanists? Undoubtedly we did; and when in due course modern historiography based on modern scholarship began its sway, mind or viewpoint or an underlying norm of judgment—call it what you will—continued to figure in every separate production exactly as before.

This needs expressly to be said because of the contrary claim regarding history-writing in our day which has recently been advanced by some historical practitioners and their attendant band of scholars. Conscious of the greater fulness and accuracy made possible by the vast accumulations of tested data put at their disposal through systematic research, they have set up as their ideal the history which represents the complete recovery of the past and is therefore that final and conclusive thing, the truth. They may admit that the truth has as yet in no single instance been attained; still they declare its mastery to be possible by reason of their confidence in the elaborate and impressive machinery of modern scholarship. Indeed, so great is their faith in this tool that they frequently call their improved method of investigation "scientific," boldly equating it with the method of the natural sciences and claiming for it an effectiveness that is bound to find its culmination in the discovery of a body of historical laws sweepingly descriptive of the past and valid for the whole future of our human kind.

As this is not the place for a searching theoretical discussion on the nature of history, we shall content ourselves with two declaratory statements which, if they prove nothing, at least make clear the position taken by the writer with regard to the above-mentioned claim. First, we agree with the champions of the "scientific" school that modern historians enjoy an immense advantage over their predecessors through the abundant factual resources made available by the extraordinarily fruitful activities of scholarship. Secondly, we flatly reject the assertion that scholarship has put us in possession of a method capable of replacing our doubts and uncertainties about the past and our incurable ignorance touching the future with a revelation carrying with it the implication of a final truth; and consequently we categorically refuse to assign to history, which has always been and must needs remain a very personal art, the status of an abstract science. . . .

FROM THE FOREWORD TO "THE GREAT ELECTOR"[3]

History in our day is so variously defined and practiced that every historian must feel moved to preface a work put out by him with a statement as to the kind of history to which he is inviting attention. In case his production is addressed in the main to his professional colleagues, he will be disposed fully to state and argumentatively to defend his choice; but if, as in the present instance, he is addressing the general reader, he will feel free to ignore the controversies agitating the academic world and to content himself with setting forth in simple declaratory terms the particular view in regard to history to which his work conforms.

Let it therefore be stated without elaboration or apology that in the present writer's view history is an accredited literary form representing a combination of scholarship and

3. Ferdinand Schevill, *The Great Elector* (Chicago: University of Chicago Press, 1947).

art. The scholarship is concerned with the recapture of past events from the surviving evidence, chiefly in the form of written documents. And here in recent generations a development has taken place which is at the bottom of much of the reigning confusion. By steadily expanding and intensifying its activity not only has scholarship assembled and made available in printed form vast fresh bodies of documents dealing with every aspect of government and society, but it has also subjected them to norms of judgment of such severity that historians, elated by these advances, have very generally been encouraged to declare that history is now able to reach conclusions as definite and final as those of the natural sciences. They have therefore not hesitated to proclaim that history as practiced by them has lost its traditional literary character and become "scientific."

The claim is so exaggerated as to invite derision; for, conceding that the latest disciples of Herodotus have at their disposal a vastly enlarged corpus of original material and that they subject it to a far more severely critical method than was formerly the case, the assertion that their conclusions have achieved a precision comparable to those of the natural sciences breaks down on even the most superficial examination. It will therefore serve an always desirable clarity to recognize that history and the natural sciences are two distinct bodies of knowledge and that each follows a particular purpose and employs an appropriate method. The equating of the two purposes and methods is the result of a defective logical analysis. The readiest way of escaping the confusion to which it leads is to abandon the false claim of "science" for the procedure of the historian and to replace it with the ancient and unobjectionable term of "scholarship."

This much agreed, let us next note that the materials assembled and sorted by scholarship are so much dead matter utterly bare of meaning until they have been reanimated by being again set in the stream of life. The stream of life is a continuous stream whose movement began with the infinitely remote first age of man and which will continue on its destined course until the unimaginable day of his extinction. Every segment of the human past, large or small, of which scholarship makes it its business to recover the surviving traces, must, in order to achieve intelligibility and significance, be again returned to the life-stream and be relived by him who undertakes to describe it. Less figuratively and more literally, the historian who by his labors as a scholar has put himself in possession of innumerable, minute, and isolated data must, as his next step, fuse them into a meaningful whole of interrelated parts. This demands his putting into play an entirely different talent from the laborious scholarly faculty. He must call on his imagination and prove himself, as far as in him lies, to be an artist.

There is a product of scholarship pure and simple: the historical monograph. Hundreds of scholars have been and are engaged in preparing these precise and detailed studies, the importance of which for the intimate penetration of the past it is impossible to exaggerate. Historical monographs are in the nature of preparatory sketches which, in spite of their great value, should not be rated as full-bodied histories; for, while performing an important service on the strict scholarship level, they do not create that intelligible whole which is the unfailing mark of the true history and which results from the mass of monographic material being fused and shaped by an individual mind.

If true history is a work of scholarship and art, it follows that, like all other works of art, it is a communication and seeks a public. Committed to this concept, the author re-affirms his earlier avowal that in writing the present history he has had in mind as audience not his professional colleagues but the broad community of cultivated men and women. While he invites the judgment of his colleagues, which in any case they will not be backward to deliver, his concern lies elsewhere, being directed to the hope that his handiwork will not be found unacceptable by the body of alert readers making up with us, as in every country of the world, the solid core of our continuing civilization. These readers may, of course, reject his offering on the unanswerable ground that it is an inferior product, a professed communication that has nothing to communicate. This would signify the author's defeat and the cancellation of his effort. But as a failure resulting from individual incompetence, it would not, it is only fair to point out, disprove the validity of the theory of history to which his work subscribes.

JAMES SCHEVILL

TABLE OF CONTENTS

THUCYDIDES

Political Philosopher and Father of Historical Method

While Herodotus' fame among men as the "Father of History" is secure beyond any possibility of eclipse, the close corporation of craftsmen who pursue history professionally has replaced him at his post of honor with his successor, Thucydides. The supersession within the narrow professional fold of the older by the younger man was so lagging a process that generations and even centuries passed before it was effected. Thucydides exercised no recognizable authority over the long line of his Greek successors except perhaps in a limited degree over Polybius. When in the Renaissance he was, as it were, exhumed from the rubble heap of classical letters, he continued to linger in Herodotus' shadow for so protracted a period that it was not until the nineteenth century that Clio's self-picked bodyguard at last resolutely set him up as their household deity. It was at that time that history experienced a remarkable rejuvenation by

1

the adoption under the leadership of Leopold Ranke and a group of German fellow workers of a critical method which held out the promise of recovering not only the true picture of the past but also the past's true significance. However, as Ranke himself was prompt to avow, the method which was stamped with his name was nothing other than the application to modern conditions of the procedure brilliantly exemplified for the first time by his Athenian predecessor of more than two thousand years before.

Although it will never cease to be a source of surprise that professional historians throughout a weary succession of centuries refused to bow to the authority of Thucydides, it is not at all surprising that Herodotus has uninterruptedly retained the public favor with which he was greeted on his first appearance. For his work, expressly named a history by him but defying exact literary classification, proved a feast of encyclopedic information spiced with delightful entertainment as welcome in our time as when it was first laid out. Readers found and still find it crammed with quickening if often dubious data on the geography and peoples of the contemporary world, interspersed with assorted tales of unbelievable horror and beguiling fairy fancy caught from the mouths of individuals encountered by the way, and offering as its main fare an account of the greatest event of the author's lifetime, the memorable crushing by the free Greeks of the assault on their liberty by the autocratic ruler of Persia.

To Thucydides, and apparently to him alone in the succeeding generation, this work of an unsystematic, romantically minded gatherer of inn and roadside gossip was a hodgepodge conferring little pleasure and inviting vigorous objections. In the opening chapter of his own work he refers unmistakably, though not by name, to his predecessor's history as a composition "attractive at truth's expense" and sharply contrasts it with his own history written "not as an essay planned to win the applause of the moment but as a possession for all time." Although Thucydides was somewhat less than a full generation removed from Herodotus, he was separated from him mentally by the gulf of one of the most sweeping revolutions of history. A born Athenian, he arrived at manhood as a finished product of that amazing culture which, like the fabled birth of Pallas Athena from the head of Zeus, had leaped to maturity as if by magic in the decades immediately following the victory of Salamis in 480 B.C.

While saturated with the rich total substance of the Athenian outlook, Thucydides' intellectual activity was particularly influenced by its rationalist ingredient. It was this element that mainly shaped the history he came to write, the *History of the Peloponnesian War*—that engrossing event of his own time, which as completely overshadowed all his days as the Greco-Persian War overshadowed the days of Herodotus. Putting aside for the moment the pattern his rationalism stamped on his own history, let us examine the attitude it caused him to develop to his predecessor's work. The admirers of Herodotus then and ever since attributed his rare storytelling skill to his childlike view of the world as a place of inexhaustible wonders. While this is unquestionably an outstanding Herodotean trait, we must be on our guard against making too much of it. For Herodotus, if endowed with something akin to the guilelessness of childhood, was also an enlightened Greek and was far from swallowing the innumerable superstitions which he stumbled

3

on in his wide travels among the Greeks and their neighbors and conscientiously recorded in his book. However, born with a curiosity which fairly matched his storytelling talent, he was prompted to make a liberal display of these strange beliefs, though generally not without a caveat to his readers as to their credibility.

It was the same with oracles. Everybody, Greeks and barbarians alike, put faith in the dark and devious pronouncements of the priests and priestesses of the more celebrated temples and particularly of the great national shrine at Delphi, and Herodotus took it as an obligation imposed by his role as inquiring reporter to record their ambiguous prophecies. Both superstitions and oracles were in the nature of digressions to the movement of the war, which is, after all, the announced subject matter of the book. Consequently they seem like annoying roadblocks to readers in our time.

Here then was material which to a rationalist like Thucydides, disburdened, as were all the advanced thinkers of his city, of superstitions, oracles, and the whole outmoded company of the Olympian gods, amounted to an invitation to re-enter the nursery from which he had happily escaped. Citizen of a town which had evolved into the most radical democracy of his and perhaps any time, he was immersed with all his energies and hopes in its palpitating concerns. Profoundly troubled by the swift shifts of public opinion and the attendant rise and fall of popular leaders, he pondered these restless phenomena through the years and gradually reached the conclusion that they took place in accordance with some hidden but ascertainable law of human nature. To this reasoning he was led in the first instance by the natural scientists (or natural philosophers as they were then called), whose earliest representatives had appeared at Miletus in Asia Minor over a hundred years before and who had arrived at remarkable discoveries in astronomy and physics predicated on this novel conception of the uniformity of nature. When in Thucydides' own generation the school of the great Hippocrates undertook to apply this stimulating doctrine to the treatment of disease, medical science promptly found itself engaged in an exciting adventure productive of a rich harvest of startling disclosures. Sharply attentive to these remarkable developments, referable in last analysis to the triumph of reason over dead custom, Thucydides came gradually to the view that the disturbing political fluctuations that characterized the Athenian domestic scene must be in accord with the nature of man, which, like the nature of the physical world of which man was an integral part, followed a determinable, ever invariable course.

However, since nothing short of the experience of a lifetime enabled him to arrive at so novel and inclusive a generalization, we are obliged to take account of his immediate government contacts, so far as the few facts we possess permit us to do so. We owe whatever knowledge we have of them to his book, in which he reports a single crucial conflict with the Athenian authorities in a few meager words characteristically bare of every emotional overtone. When in the year 424, the seventh year of the war, the Spartan general Brasidas laid siege to Amphipolis, an Athenian dependency in the province of Thrace, Thucydides, raised by public vote to the command of a small fleet of no more than seven vessels, was ordered to relieve the town. But on his approach he learned that it had already surrendered. For his failure to perform what was probably an impossible feat he was impulsively punished with banishment by the Athenian people in general assembly and spent the following twenty years, that is, until the defeat and surrender of Athens, beyond the bounds of the Athenian empire.

The sentence, darkly tragic for himself, proved a boon to posterity, inasmuch as it enabled him single-mindedly to pursue a purpose which, according to his own avowal, he had formed at the very outbreak of the war. He resolved to write a history of the war in the conviction that it was certain to be, as was later proved to be the case, the greatest convulsion that had ever shaken the Greek world. An exile, roaming at pleasure beyond the limits of his native city, he was free to inquire into the events of the prolonged and cumulatively ferocious civil struggle and critically to weigh the many contradictory versions of them he was able to gather, preferably from the leading participants themselves.

It is interesting to speculate as to when Thucydides turned from the primary business of note-taking to the subsequent task of composition. While still in exile did he begin to shape his data into a connected narrative? So tightly is the work fused from a single unvarying angle that we are bound to dismiss the conjecture of one or more tentative starts in favor of the view that he did not begin composition until, with the war brought to its close in the year 404, he was able to return to his humbled city deprived, as a sign of defeat, of its defensive walls but still crowned with the symbol of its enduring glory, the towering Acropolis.

Because the *History of the Peloponnesian War* breaks off abruptly with the year 411, that is, seven years before its actual termination, we are obliged to conclude that Thu-

6

cydides died while still immersed in his labors, although we are left without a confirmatory statement on his death from any contemporary source. A reasonably safe conjecture would seem to be that he lived briefly into the next, that is, the fourth century B.C. and (assuming his birth in 455 B.C.) died at an age between fifty-five and sixty years. The first descriptive statement that his uncompleted work imperatively calls for is that it is strictly and narrowly a political history. In the light of his already noted derogatory reference to the garrulous, wide-ranging Herodotus, this should cause no surprise. Pre-eminently a politician and a student of politics, he found it natural and easy to limit himself to the field of government and war in his presentation of the course pursued by the several large and small city-states of the Greek world during the long man-and-wealth-devouring civil struggle in which Sparta and Athens played the part of the leading protagonists.

We may regret Thucydides' decision to confine his history within the indicated bounds, even while freely conceding his right to do so. Many of his admirers, including the present writer, would have welcomed a broad cultural history from his hand devoted to the exposition of the incomparable achievements of the Greek world, and particularly of his own Athens, in every field of human endeavor. And let no one say that such a work lay beyond Thucydides' powers. True, his leading interest was undoubtedly politics, but that he was a man in full possession of the rounded culture of the age may be gathered from the whole tone of his writing and gains conviction from the famous canvas of total Athenian achievement unrolled in the funeral oration he put in the mouth of Pericles. However, his failure to write a book

7

other than the one he chose to write cannot by any stretch of a critic's privilege be charged to him as a fault.

If we now inquire into the reasons that moved him to narrow the story of the war to its political concerns, the answer has already been suggested by the revelation of his lifelong concentration on the problem of government and his conviction that the apparently unaccountable Athenian fluctuations in the area of both domestic and foreign policy become explicable on the assumption of a hidden constant, identifiable as human nature. Observe that he did not occupy himself with the operation of human nature in the strictly individual enterprise of art and letters. What exclusively pricked his curiosity was human behavior when various, originally distinct, social units had been drawn into the close coherence of statehood. These constitutive social units would be opposed but interdependent interest groups moved to join together by the ever pressing need for mutual protection. However, even when hotly cultivating, in the interest of survival, the idealist sentiment of togetherness called patriotism, they would engage in sharp contention with one another for the control of their total power located in the recent creation of the state. The governing council of the state, whether special and limited in character as in the case of an oligarchy or inclusive and general as in the case of a democracy, was the normal battlefield of that struggle, and the measure finally carried would be a reflection of the opinion of the victor group. What troubled and distressed Thucydides about the procedure was not the procedure itself, which accorded with his master concept of human nature, but that, in the democracies at least, the adopted measure was so lightly regarded that the injection of a new event into the situation, often on the day after an apparently unalterable decision had been taken, frequently sufficed to cause that decision to be revised and even reversed.

Since no society can function healthily and effectively in a perpetual flux, Thucydides faced the problem of how that flux could be steadied without destroying the democracy to which he, together with the vast majority of his fellow Athenians, was committed. It has sometimes been affirmed that he dwelt so above the battle and maintained so detached an attitude to the events he described that he failed to disclose the form of government that enjoyed his personal preference. To hold this opinion is to read him with completely closed eyes and mind. Through his unobtrusive manner rather than by direct avowal, he declared in the most unambiguous language that he was opposed, on the one hand, to the rule of a wealthy upper crust, that is, to oligarchy and, on the other hand, to that extreme or frenzied democracy indistinguishable from mob rule. He was, in brief, a moderate democrat and, as such, favored the participation of the whole citizen body in the affairs of government, subject—and the reservation is crucial—to the guidance of high-minded, intelligent leaders inflexibly devoted to the good of the community as a whole and prepared, if necessary, to meet head-on the panicky stampede to which the herded mass, whether of men or sheep, has always been prone.

More than once he pointed out that Pericles was a leader of this desirable kind, who by his authoritative sway of the general assembly, the *ecclesia,* won its consent to measures by which he exercised, in effect, a form of personal rule. When on the death of Pericles such irresponsible demagogues as Cleon, the tanner, came to dominate the assembly

9

and lured it onto the path of headlong adventure, he leaves
no possible doubt that in his opinion it was the decline from
wisely inspired leadership to its selfishly directed opposite,
and therefore not balanced democracy but its unbalanced
excess, that slowly and inescapably brought Athens to its
knees.

It is illuminating to compare this firm allegiance to democratic principle by the "earth-born" Thucydides with its con-
temptuous rejection by his somewhat younger contemporary, the "sky-born" philosopher Plato. Let us not fail to
recall in this connection that to the world in general, and
particularly to its educated upper stratum, Plato to this day
represents the finest flowering of the radiant Athenian culture. Plato, like Thucydides, was persuaded that the defeat
of Athens in the course of the long war had resulted from
the taking over of its government by irresponsible and
shameless demagogues. But here their agreement ended. If
Thucydides, as we have seen, resolutely refused to toss democracy overboard, it was because he held that, though the
liberty it implied had been betrayed by evil men, still it constituted the indispensable setting for the nobly creative society which Athens had achieved. How different Plato's reaction to liberty became on the defeat of Athens is well
known. In his view liberty had proved itself so false an ideal
that it would have to be abandoned in its entirety in favor
of the opposite principle of order—indeed, of so tight an order that there would not remain the tiniest crack for liberty
to slip through. For this amazing project he reached in *The
Republic* and certain related writings above the earth into
the sky, where were to be found, enthroned like worshipful
goddesses, the perfect archetypes of the imperfect forms of

objects among which man spent his fumbling life below. He ended by devising a state in which movement, the spontaneous and ever faithful attendant of liberty, was forbidden and in which each citizen practiced a skill or was assigned an occupation determined by his aptitude and education. The crowning imposition, comparable in authority to a Mosaic commandment, was that the citizen body was required to live together in happy harmony under the rule of officials, called Guardians, empowered to punish every deviation from the established system, if necessary, with death.

This program, as everyone will at once recognize, was a blueprint for the kind of totalitarian state of which we have had outstanding realizations in our time. And let no one say that, had Plato's projected republic been actually realized, it would have been very different from the totalitarian states of which the living generation has had a terrifying experience, for the simple and sufficient reason that Plato was a kindly dreamer who dwelt at the opposite moral pole from some of our modern dictators. Plato's system neither would nor could have been different, since, however ideally planned, it was to be operated by a collective executive, the above-named Guardians, as absolute in its power as the Russian Politburo and as certain to perpetuate itself and its iron-clad system by resorting to all the inhuman horrors with which the totalitarian regimes of our day have frozen our blood.

At the side of this picture of an exaggerated program of order may be set the no less repulsive picture of an exaggerated state of liberty to which Athens and many another Greek city had unhappily succumbed in the course of the Peloponnesian War. Must we not conclude that, theoretically viewed, the two opposed systems devour each other and that

11

their mutual cancellation may be hailed as a convincing argument for the golden mean, for that balance between liberty and order which was advocated by Plato's pupil Aristotle and which, as a glance down the ages will show, has the indorsement of the massed evidence of history. It was precisely this balance of opposites which Thucydides upheld when, in spite of the ruin wrought by liberty without order, he advocated liberty under responsible leaders in the deep persuasion that it alone was able to create a prosperous civilization and its indispensable associate, the open society. What a shrunken figure Plato cuts at his side with his dream state planned as an escape from the perils of liberty and organized as a rigidly closed society in which the merest hint of change was reckoned a crime and a sacrilege.

With the preliminaries behind us which should clear the path to a better understanding of Thucydides, let us turn to the *History* itself. It falls into two kinds of material which, while related, are still so sharply differentiated as to call for separate consideration. The two kinds are, first, the narrative of events, which make up about three-fourths of the text and, second, the speeches by leading participants in the struggle, which make up the remaining fourth.

In the first chapter of Book i Thucydides offers a statement of such importance that it must be quoted in full. On the narrative of events, which we shall consider first, he says: "Far from permitting myself to derive it from the first source that came to hand, I did not even trust my own impressions. It rests partly on what I saw myself, partly on what others saw for me, the accuracy of the report being tried always by the most severe and detailed tests possible.

My conclusions have cost me some labor from the want of coincidence among accounts of the same occurrences by different eyewitnesses, arising sometimes from imperfect memory, sometimes from undue partiality for one side or the other. The absence of romance in my history [this with a side glance at Herodotus!] will, I fear, detract somewhat from its interest; but if it be judged useful for those inquirers who desire an exact knowledge of the past as an aid to the interpretation of the future, which in the course of human events must resemble it, I shall be content."

The statement supplies the justification for hailing Thucydides as the Father of Historical Method. True, he got his facts from oral witnesses, to whom modern historians have assigned a much lower rating as reliable sources of information than to contemporary documents. However, documents were not available in the age of Thucydides, except a very limited group of intercity treaties and some laws and incidents, chiefly battles, whose importance had led them to be noted on tablets of stone. Nor were books available apart from a few writings in the nature of pamphlets on current constitutional issues. And, of course, there were no newspapers. This explains not only our author's expensive and laborious procedure of traveling about to interrogate eyewitnesses but also his complaint of their unreliability. Consequently, the critical acumen that enabled him to reduce the conflicting reports to a common mean which has ever since been accepted as an approximately correct image of the actual event is all the more remarkable. If we agree, as we must, that the inescapable injection of something of Thucydides' personality into the picture he presents signifies that it is not to be accepted as the final and absolute truth, his case does not differ by a hair's breadth from that of his modern successor who, on turning to composition after having burrowed into a heaped mountain of published and unpublished documents, can no more escape from introducing a subjective and evaluating element into his work than could Thucydides. Even though the notion of an absolute historical truth continues to haunt the mind of some followers of history, it is indubitably passing out of favor as a feasible professional ideal and being replaced by a search for an approximate truth as close to the actual event as honest inquiry and a disciplined rational mentality can achieve.

While the success with which Thucydides pursued his own inquiry has won him a reputation beyond praise for honesty, intelligence, and critical penetration, he faced other difficulties besides the conflicting character of his evidence. Among these the absence of a usable calendar has for present-day readers, at least, proved to be the most disturbing. All the Greek city-states reckoned the year in lunar months but failed to agree on the month to be counted as the first of the year. When the various three-hundred-and-sixty-day calendars departed too manifestly from the familiar succession of seasons spun by the solar year, the spread was corrected by adding a month to the lunar year. Rejecting these conflicting systems as impractical for a book addressed to the whole Greek world, Thucydides invented a calendar of his own, which named 431 B.C., the year of the outbreak of the war, as year 1 and divided the year, in accordance with Greek campaigning practices, into two seasons—summer and winter.

Although this calendar enabled Thucydides to impress on

his work a measure of desirable chronological precision, it
also imposed a serious handicap. Since the Peloponnesian
War was an agony felt throughout the whole Greek world
down to its remotest village, the events which Thucydides
felt impelled to note swelled to a veritable flood. Centrally
or peripherally located, important or unimportant, they had
by his system to be yoked together according to the year of
their occurrence. It is a little amusing and more than a little
sad that some pages of this author, who was the chief impetus to contemporary historical method, should read like
an anticipation by over a thousand years of the dull chronicle form of the Middle Ages.

Happily the drop to the medieval level was sufficiently rare
for the boring pages it produced to be swiftly forgotten
among the innumerable palpitating incidents that make up
the bulk of the book. Occasionally, however, even the most
dramatic episodes had their glitter dimmed by their presentation in separate annual instalments. A case in point is the
story of Plataea, as inherently significant as any the war
produced. From 431 to 427, that is, through the first four
years of the conflict, this little town, an ally and protectorate
of Athens on the Boeotian frontier, was assaulted by the
Thebans with the support of their Peloponnesian allies.
With heroic resolution the Plataeans supported their cause
through four exhausting campaigns only to find themselves,
on having dwindled to a few hundred starving defenders, at
last obliged to surrender. The mockery of a trial which preceded their cold-blooded butchery is one of the most darkly
cynical and humanly revolting pages of the book. This
fourth and last section, together with the three preceding
sections into which the Plataean episode is broken up, sup-

ply examples of narrative different in kind but of an equal excellence in manner. However, it can only be regretted that the repeated interruption of a unified, breath-taking incident slows down its vital movement.

Let no one entertain the idea that the occasional decline of effectiveness imposed by the confining calendar seriously challenges our estimate of Thucydides as a narrative artist. Whenever he leaps into action with unchecked vigor he gives us scenes of unrivaled power. The pages bearing the name of Mitylene (Book iii, chap. 9) display such a scene, as do also the events headlined with the two associated place names of Pylos and Sphacteria (Book iv, chap. 12). The climax is reached with the Sicilian expedition, which constitutes the exclusive theme of Books vi and vii and sets forth with an exceptional richness of detail what turned out to be the culminating episode of the war. It has probably elicited a warmer chorus of praise from competent critics than has ever been raised over a similar work. Macaulay called it the *ne plus ultra* of human art, and John Stuart Mill declared that it was the most powerful piece of narrative writing perhaps in all literature.

It is their unbroken flow and narrative compactness that cause the two above-named Sicilian books to stand out as the crowning feature of the history. In a concealed but hardly accidental manner they present themselves to view as being, besides an animated story, an allegory of the war and the fated destruction of Athens cast in dramatic form. No tragedian of the contemporary stage opened his piece with a more ominously joyful scene than that with which Thucydides introduced his Sicilian tragedy. Who, having read it, can ever forget the picture of the vast Athenian armament sailing forth from Piraeus in single file with all the ships' crews at the voice of a herald simultaneously pouring libations for a prosperous voyage from gold and silver goblets. The reader, in contrast to the elated shipmates, feels to the marrow the hovering doom which visibly gathers over the exultant adventurers' heads as their troubles fall on them thick as hail among the hostile Sicilians and their bodies and souls alike are slowly ground to dust by the mills of the gods offended by an arrogance forbidden to the lowly race of men.

Since readers who lack the interest or the inclination to read the whole work of Thucydides have frequently had the Sicilian expedition recommended to them as affording a view of the author at the height of his powers, a few words of counsel addressed to such abbreviators may promote both understanding and enjoyment. So great a number of geographical terms, most of them no longer current—rivers, promontories, coasts, towns—occur in the text that it is imperative in order intelligently to follow the movement of events to have immediately at hand the best attainable map of the contemporary Greek world. This precaution imposes itself in consequence of our historian's wise and unwearying attention to geographical detail. However, since his geographical abundance is no more than a derivative feature of his characteristic total devotion to historical actuality, it is indispensable for the reader to be himself at least measurably addicted to historical detail if he is to extract an adequate reward from the complicated unfolding of the three-year campaign on land and sea that the Athenians directed to the capture of Syracuse before their effort terminated in their total failure and unexampled destruction.

While the technical and professional command Thucydides exhibits in describing the successive naval battles which took place in the almost completely landlocked harbor of Syracuse tend to establish the conviction that he must have had training as a naval expert—a conviction fortified by the single known fact of his public career, his failure as admiral of an Athenian fleet to relieve Amphipolis—more striking still than this professionalism is his impressive rendering of the fluctuating state of mind of the excited combatants throughout the ever renewed harbor fight. The summit of the contained artistry (a term happily expressive of the compact stylistic quality of this historian) is reached with the tragic attempted land retreat of the broken Athenian army and the unforgettable story of its extinction under the smothering attack of its swarming foes.

On turning to the speeches, we again set out by citing Thucydides' own statement about them: "With reference to the speeches in this history, some were delivered before the war began, others while it was going on; some I heard myself, others I got from various quarters. It was in all cases difficult to carry them word for word in one's memory so that my habit has been to make the speakers say what was in my opinion demanded of them by the various occasions, of course adhering as closely as possible to the general sense of what was really said."

In introducing speeches into his history, Thucydides was following a precedent set by Herodotus, and he must have adopted the practice the more readily since it fell in with a characteristic feature of the argumentative Greek mentality. It so little characterizes our modern mental habits that the present-day reader is obliged to make something of an effort to meet it with an open mind. However, having overcome his initial distaste and let himself be absorbed into the substance of the Thucydidean speeches, it is more than likely that he will end by conceding them a significance quite equal to that of the narrative of events. Unendowed with the reflective turn of thought of his successor, Herodotus enveloped the events he recorded with a wreath of no more than mildly clarifying speeches. The historians who came after Thucydides throughout the long succession of classical centuries were so hypnotized by what they considered the charms of rhetoric that they tended to hide and even black out the facts they had set out to present behind a blinding curtain of verbal fireworks. It has been universally agreed that the speeches of Thucydides carry so different a content from those of all other classical historians that they rate as a contribution unique of its kind.

Among Thucydidean scholars, especially among those of the most recent vintage, the speeches have been the subject of lively debate. This is understandable in view of certain questions they inescapably raise. With Thucydides himself admitting his inability to acquire satisfactory transcripts and his consequent practice of making the speakers say what in his opinion the occasion required, the question naturally arises how much of each speech belonged to the orator and how much to his helpful historical sponsor. And since no conclusive solution of this conundrum is possible, a great variety of answers has been suggested, ranging all the way from the simple acceptance of the speeches as genuine products of the spokesmen to whom they are attributed to the radical view that the nominal speakers are no better than mouthpieces for the free compositions of Thucydides. The present writer rejects both of these extreme positions and holds to the middle ground set forth by Thucydides himself, that, while letting himself be guided by what he could learn of the actual speeches, he provided the form in which they appear. Although some of the speeches can hardly be brought under this compromise formula, since it would seem impossible for Thucydides to have received any account whatever of them, the proposed moderate view may still be recommended, not only because it takes account of the complicated factors involved, but also because it pays proper respect to a historian who was determined to give his readers the best he had.

The question as to the distribution of the purely factual content of the speeches between Thucydides and the several speakers is not particularly significant. What alone really matters is the form in which the speeches appear, and the form is indisputably the handiwork of Thucydides. The verdict lies beyond the reach of challenge because the speeches are cast unmistakably and throughout in an unvarying style without the faintest attempt to stamp on them the individual quality of the speakers to whom they are ascribed. It is this style, an intimately personal utterance without a trace of kinship with the conventional rhetorical adornment so characteristic of the post-Thucydidean histories of the classical age, that gives them their weight and value; and it is precisely from the presence of Thucydides himself in the speeches that we derive our knowledge of his view of the origin and significance of the war and are acquainted with his reflections on politics, constituting in their sum his philosophy of history.

We shall find it convenient to review the speeches in associated groups and to chose as our first group the speeches delivered at Sparta and Athens, respectively, immediately before and after the outbreak of the war (Book i, chaps. 3 and 5). The occasion for the speeches made at Sparta was furnished by the appearance in that city of an ambassador from Corinth charged with pricking the slow-moving Lacedaemonians to action against the continuing aggressions of Athens. The orator brilliantly contrasted the conservative temper of the inland, agrarian Spartans with the enterprising spirit of the outgoing, commercial Athenians and summed up the latter's disturbing role in the overcrowded Greek fish pond with the charge: "The Athenians are addicted to innovation. They take no rest themselves and give none to others."

In rejoinder the Athenian ambassador, on being invited to speak, was content to review with ill-concealed haughtiness the glorious role played by his city in liberating the Greek world from the Persian menace and to claim that by reason of that service the Athenian empire was rightfully acquired. But it was at Athens itself and by Pericles, chief architect of the Athenian empire, that the Lacedaemonians had hurled straight back into their faces the diplomatic ultimatum in which they demanded that the Athenians promptly and without delay renounce their empire and humbly accept their reduction to the earlier equality with their Greek city neighbors which they had presumptuously abandoned.

Clearly audible beneath the voices of these several speakers is the voice of Thucydides himself disclosing in cool, dispassionate terms his view of the impending crisis. Athens in his opinion had been engaged in unifying the Greek world

21

composed of scores of petty sovereignties engaged in un-ceasing ruinous strife with one another, and with this policy of pacification and consolidation he found no fault. How-ever, since this was manifestly a policy of the kind we now call imperialism and which was directed at the supersession of the ancient tradition of unlimited sovereignty exercised by all alike, it aroused an all but universal resistance of which Sparta, the immobile military community of the Pelo-ponnese, became the acknowledged leader. Not for a mo-ment did Thucydides delude himself into believing that the violent clash of program and temper that imperialism produced could be resolved by any means other than war. And not only does he let it be implied but he expressly de-clares that it was Sparta and her allies who unleashed the war because it was the only measure remaining to them for putting a stop to the Athenian piecemeal absorption of the Greek world.

War thereupon followed, its opening action consisting in the invasion in 431 B.C. of Attica by the Lacedaemonian army. When the first campaign had come to an end, Peri-cles held the obligatory funeral oration over the Athenian dead. Profoundly moved in heart and spirit, he seized the occasion to retrace for his hearers the ground traversed by Athens since the great naval victory of Salamis over Persian Xerxes. Exultantly he affirmed as the earliest beginning of the magnificent national transformation the free and adven-turous spirit that had taken possession of the whole popula-tion. Then, in resounding words that have rung down the centuries, he described the commercial and industrial ex-pansion of the city, passing on from there to the attendant spiritual development, of which the immortal achievements

22

in the arts were the living witness. He concluded with words that swelled like a boast but were no more than the plain, unvarnished truth that this city had fashioned the cultural pattern for the whole Greek world.

Without diminishing by a shade the glory redounding to Pericles for the oratorical picture he drew of Athens at the height of its power, we may yet insist that this picture was at least as much the creation of Thucydides as his own. And what is the inescapable meaning of this identification of the historian with the vision of the statesman? Thucydides thereby renewed and deepened the view of the national crisis which he had formed even before war broke out, and by this avowal committed himself afresh, and in the most solemn manner, to the imperialist role which fate had thrust upon the city of his birth.

We shall next take note of another group of speeches, which in their sum are in the sharpest conceivable contrast with those just reviewed. This particular group belongs to the period after the death of Pericles (in 429 B.C.), when the demagogues had taken over and slowly scattered to the winds every hope Thucydides had ever entertained that the war would be fought through to a conclusion representing a higher level of rational organization. The speakers of this group were all Athenians; and while each represented a program emphatically his own, the total consequence of the policies in debate at the time was an ever darkening chaos. Pre-eminent among these muddlers were Cleon and Alcibiades. Cleon was a tanner by trade who, shortly after the death of Pericles, gained an evil authority over the Athenian masses by his flattery of their passion for military glory. He did not reign long, for he was killed in battle in 424. However, his departure from the scene brought no relief, since he was presently succeeded by a much more talented corrupter of public morals. This was Alcibiades, a young man of great charm of manner and outstanding ability and an offspring, besides, of the oldest aristocracy of the land. It is these features that account for the consideration he received in his day and has enjoyed ever since, although he spread an even deeper confusion than Cleon and made a larger contribution to the final catastrophe of his native city than all the Spartan generals taken together.

Two of the several speeches of Alcibiades should under no circumstances be passed over. In the first of these (Book vi, chap. 18) he appears as the lighthearted proponent of the Sicilian expedition, the risks of which he represents as negligible. In the second speech (Book vi, chap. 20), which he delivered before the Spartan assembly after his dismissal from the army and escape to the enemy's camp, he pointed out and earnestly urged the measures which would infallibly bring about the total ruin of Athens. The voice we hear in these two addresses is that of an arrogant, irresponsible, self-seeking, basically vulgar aristocrat to whom the unobtrusive art of Thucydides concedes the privilege of letting him hang himself by means of a deadly self-portrait.

The speeches attributed by Thucydides to Cleon and Alcibiades are psychological masterpieces. By the revelation they afford of the working of the speakers' minds, they supply a political clue without which the accompanying narrative of events would hardly have risen above the level of a conscientious almanac. Not by as much as a whispered word did Thucydides betray the contempt he must have felt for these wreckers of the Athenian cause; not by even a veiled hint did he depart from his stern guiding principle of letting the facts speak for themselves with the minimum intrusion into the record of the personality of the narrator.

Because the leaders of the Athenian assembly were, after all, not all men of the corrupt order of Cleon and Alcibiades, it is desirable to pay some attention to the speeches of Diodotus and Nicias, two men of a continuing high-minded outlook. Both not only dared openly to confront the un-abashed demagogues but also demonstrated that the ancient virtues of the citizen had not entirely vanished under the mounting tide of public immorality. Thoroughly worth reading is the address by which the humane Diodotus caused an appalling motion carried by Cleon to be reversed in just the nick of time. The business before the popular assembly at the moment was what to do about allied Mitylene, a town on the island of Lesbos. After rising in revolt, it had in 427 B.C. been again reduced to obedience. Making him-self the mouthpiece of the mob's unbridled appetite for re-venge, Cleon had disastrously put through the resolution that the whole adult male population of Mitylene should be put to the sword and the women and children sold into slavery. Only by the courageous intervention of Diodotus was the unbelievable decree recalled (Book iii, chap. 9). In the Mitylene speeches of Cleon and Diodotus, Thucydides gives another impressive example of his masterly understanding of party politics and the incalculable vagaries of ultra-democratic procedure.

Nicias, a worthy man and citizen and also the general in command, was as unfortunate as he was incapable of the disastrous Sicilian expedition. While Thucydides, the Athenian patriot, must have both admired and pitied him, he remained true to his unwavering historical code which forbade him to mingle fact-based judgment with personal feeling. The text carries several speeches Nicias delivered, some to the Athenian assembly, some to the unhappy army under his command in Sicily. By these invariably honest and invariably uninspiring orations, Thucydides permits Nicias to draw his own portrait, which is as strikingly realized in its hopeless mediocrity as is the criminal portrait Alcibiades obligingly gives of himself.

Although difficult to classify because it represents a factional debate rather than speeches, no admirer of Thucydides can bring himself to terminate the consideration of this feature of his history without including the so-called "Melian debate" (Book v, chap. 17). This debate turned, as we shall see, on the issue of imperialism, and since the two recent world wars may be regarded as a ferocious uninterrupted debate on this identical issue, the Melian debate has frequently been extracted from the Thucydidean text and set high on a pedestal for everyone to marvel at as an exposition of the imperialist theme as valid in the twentieth century as it was when it was set down over two thousand years ago.

Melos was an Aegean island which had refused to join the Athenian empire because it preferred neutrality, and it preferred neutrality because it was a Lacedaemonian colony. Also to be considered is that, while secretly inclining to Sparta, it could not and did not look for active support from the homeland because it was situated in waters dominated by the Athenian navy. Long irritated by this neutral stand and seduced at last by the offensive policy championed by Alcibiades, the Athenians resolved in 416 to bring Melos to heel by military action. Having gained a foothold on the island, they opened negotiations with a Melian commission over the question of surrender. While it is difficult to the point of impossibility to believe that the exchange of views among the two opposed delegations proceeded in the orderly manner indicated by Thucydides, he constructs a debate between a ruthless power frankly resting its case on naked might and a puny victim pleading for an abstract right without the backing of even a remotely sufficient amount of military power to sustain its position.

The debate ended exactly as have the innumerable similar debates before and since. The stubborn Melians refused to bend their necks to the threat of force, and a conflict followed which the Athenians won. Thucydides reports the upshot in these words: "The Athenians put to death all the grown men and sold the women and children into slavery." With this monstrous conquest followed in the next year by the Sicilian expedition, the Athenian imperialism entered on its final and frenzied stage and died of its own excess. Thucydides plainly believed that a moderate, rational imperialism was a possibility and might have been crowned in the end with an enduring peaceful organization of the bitterly divided Greek world.

It remains to extract from Thucydides' book his philosophy of history, which can only approximate, in the main, with what we may more inclusively call his philosophy of life. Not for a moment can we be in doubt that its root was an unshaken faith in human energy and movement. Their unhampered exercise was predicated on a substantial but not unlimited measure of freedom accorded both to the individual citizen and to the political societies the citizens had been obliged to establish in order to survive. We have already mentioned the undeviating dedication of Thucydides to this limited freedom and have learned that, in spite of its tragic change at Athens into unchecked license, he was persuaded not to abandon it as an essential element of his social outlook. Another feature of that outlook was the elimination of the still popularly held view of the capricious intervention of the Olympian gods in human affairs. This in his eyes was a superstitious hocus-pocus which had been swept away, like dusty cobwebs, by a succession of scientific thinkers who, by tireless study of the processes of nature, had shown that the only effective tool for penetrating nature's close-kept secrets was the hitherto grossly neglected human faculty of reason. From the scientists Thucydides took over their basic rationalism, accepting it, after his rejection of the outmoded divinities, as the only instrument available to man for the proud fashioning of his earthly destiny.

Movement, liberty, rationalism—these three articles of faith make up the substance of Thucydides' philosophy of life and history and provided him with the solid ground on which to rest his ruling thought about the Peloponnesian War. When the prolonged Greek crisis finally took the shape of a duel between Athens and Sparta, he could not, possessed of his broad-minded civic outlook, have felt even a moment's hesitation as to where he stood. His private and personal outlook was essentially identical with the outlook of Athens. Its stark opposite was the outlook of Sparta, characterized by immobility, fixed order, and irrational tradition. It is not surprising therefore that at the very beginning of his history he indicated that in his opinion Sparta was a holdover from

a past age and doomed to disappear. That conviction, however, did not prevent this man of an unfailing equanimity
from acknowledging certain undeniable elements of strength
inherent in the Spartan system. He paid his respect to the
discipline and steadiness of the Spartan commonwealth and
never yielded in the slightest degree to the prompting he
must occasionally have felt to deflate the awed deference
with which the whole contemporary world viewed Spartan
military prowess. No general of his own Athens ever received more admiring attention from him than Spartan
Brasidas, and this in spite of the fact that it was Brasidas
who captured Amphipolis and was the immediate instrument of Thucydides' political disgrace. It is plain that what
caught Thucydides' fancy about Brasidas was that he had
cast off the Spartan provincial dulness and that he boasted a
swift intelligence and employed a novel military tactic of a
daring that represented a complete reversal of the habitual
Spartan mentality. In the end it was the antiquated Spartan
principles that carried the day over the more vital but cor-
rupted principles of Athens. This development Thucydides
did not hesitate explicitly to set forth, but in doing so he did
not surrender his abiding faith in the defeated principles
whenever fearlessly and uncompromisingly practiced.

We noted at the outset that Thucydides narrowed his
conception of history to politics and that his resolution may
confidently be explained by his eager concentration throughout his life on the government of Athens. We also noted
that, having become persuaded by a long line of scientific
observers of the uniformity of nature and of the unfailing
presence in nature of law, he concluded that the clashes he
observed among the constituent social groups of Athens for

political control fell under an identical compulsion. He called this compulsion the law of human nature and insisted on its perpetual effectiveness because it was his faith that human nature never changed. It was owing to this conviction that he ventured to recommend to all seekers of political wisdom his exact and truthful presentation of the past as an infallible clue to the understanding of the future.

By adding this political philosophy to his larger philosophy of life within which it was embraced, we come close to what we may call the quintessence of Thucydides. Much more clearly than in his own lifetime or in all the succeeding centuries down to our time, it has disclosed itself to the living generation of men and won their unstinted admiration. Convincing proof of the ever waxing favor of Thucydides is supplied by the spate of books on him that in recent years has poured from the presses of the Western world. The masculine vigor of his thought linked to his exemplary exhibition of what present-day historians accept as the earliest instance of a scientific method of investigation has become a light leading to his professional following, and his influence has not failed to penetrate beyond the narrow group of historical practitioners into every broadly humane circle of Europe and America. In the vast crisis which at this moment hangs darkening over the world, the credo of the free individual and the free society, so valorously sustained by Thucydides, is confronted with as deadly a threat as ever before in history. What wonder therefore that his ghost, which like every noble ghost that ever lived still walks the earth, has joined the ranks of freedom sworn to resist to their last breath the onset of the massed slaves of any totalitarian tyrant.

BIBLIOGRAPHICAL NOTE

The text of the *Peloponnesian War* used is that of the Modern Library, New York. Book and chapter numbers refer to this text. The few titles entered here owe their listing to the fact that they conspicuously contributed to the author's understanding of a complicated period in classical history. John H. Finley, Jr., *Thucydides* (Cambridge, Mass.: Harvard University Press, 1942); Charles N. Cochrane, *Thucydides and the Science of History* (London: Oxford University Press, 1929); A. W. Gomme, *Essays in Greek History and Literature* (Oxford: Basil Blackwell, 1937); Werner Jaeger, *Paideia: The Ideals of Greek Culture*, translated from the second German edition by Gilbert Highet, Vol. I: *Archaic Greece: The Mind of Athens* (London: Oxford University Press, 1945).

ST. AUGUSTINE

Destroyer and Preserver

By universal consent St. Augustine is the towering figure in the early history of Christianity in the Latin West. It is equally undisputed that he had a larger share in fashioning the creed and organization of the Roman Catholic church than any other Christian Father. Far from suffering eclipse on the coming of the Reformation, he was, on account of his unwavering insistence on faith as the exclusive door to the approach of God, appropriated by the Protestants as their master light. Consequently he won and to this day enjoys the same commanding position with them as with the Mother Church.

It is not the purpose of the present study to treat of St. Augustine in the exalted role of founder that he holds with both Catholics and Protestants, nor is it proposed to examine the philosophical and theological contributions which are the steppingstones of the spiritual eminence he attained. The writer's plan has a far more restricted scope and stems from his vocation as a secular historian naturally and legitimately curious about such works of St. Augustine as to some degree encroach on secular matters, however far they may be from ruling secular intent. In the vast literary production of the great Western Father there are two, and precisely his two most famous works, which are definitely charged with matters of a worldly nature. They are the *Confessions* and the *City of God*. It is proposed in this study to weigh them in the same scale as the works of men who, lacking the ecclesiastical stamp and the concentrated religious outlook of St. Augustine, define themselves as indubitable secular historians. True, the two indicated works are so steeped in a single-minded concern with religion that they will always remain separated as by an ocean's width from both ancient and modern historical works. Nevertheless in one way or another they so definitely contain material extending beyond the boundary of religion that no reasonable objection can be lodged against bringing them into juxtaposition with admittedly secular histories and evaluating them by the same criteria.

St. Augustine was born A.D. 354 in a region which is now French Tunis and which was then the eastern section of the Roman province of Africa. Thus born an "African," he gladly identified himself as such by an all but uninterrupted residence in his homeland. He received the current education of the period at Carthage, the leading African city. This signified the study of Latin grammar and literature together with what by his own statement could not have amounted to more than a smattering of Greek. However, several philosophies, propounded by a succession of Greek thinkers and translated into Latin, figured prominently in the curriculum.

Although at the time of St. Augustine's birth Christianity had been an officially recognized religion of the Roman Empire for a quarter of a century, paganism still dominated the educational system and retained a strong hold on the population. This fluid situation was reflected in the young man's family. His mother, Monica, had become a confirmed, dedicated Christian, while his father continued to hold firmly to the pagan faith and practices. The mother's influence was great enough to secure for the boy a measure of Christian background as a catechumen, but the new teaching had so little lure for him that he eagerly embraced the pagan instruction to which he was directed by his father.

We owe this information to the *Confessions* which St. Augustine wrote in his middle years following his conversion to Christianity. Taken together with similar personal comments scattered unsystematically throughout the book, this explains how it came about that the work has often been subtitled an autobiography. However, the autobiographical items are so few and so casually injected into the text that it is decidedly misleading to regard them as sufficient for what is commonly called an autobiography, except for the single purpose running like a silver thread through the book—the tracing of the hesitant steps by which the skeptically minded scholar broke away from his pagan moorings and opened his mind and heart to the Christian illumination.

To the present-day secular reader the rarity of authentic autobiographical data in the *Confessions* will always be a source of sharp disappointment. Even the foregoing family data are vaguely adumbrated rather than clearly set forth. On the author's next taking up the story of his adolescent years, he offers a fairly lively account of the various transgressions which he and his youthful playmates thoughtlessly committed. In the chastening which followed his conversion, he magnified these petty derelictions into unquestionable sins, although no appraisal of them by a modern commentator would rate them as other than the pranks and breaches of the social order inseparable through all the ages of man from the process of juvenile adjustment to the ruling mores.

While in this casual manner we are at least given the flavor of the saint's immediate boyhood atmosphere, we are not favored with as much as a single line on the civil society of his native province or on the government of the state of which his province was a part. This is a particularly keen cause of regret, since the state to which he owed allegiance was the Roman Empire, whose government and society were at the time smitten with a blight which, begun many generations before, had by the fourth century A.D. reached an acceleration clearly prophetic of their early complete dissolution. With his penetrating intelligence and powerful moral bent St. Augustine was incomparably fitted to give us an eyewitness account of the breakup of the Roman social and political structure. But he rejected the opportunity, rejected it in so sweeping a manner that we would not even know that he was a subject of the disintegrating state were it not for the rare and purely accidental naming of an emperor or some lesser governmental official.

The *Confessions* are not properly classifiable as autobiography in the accepted meaning of the word. Even a swift preliminary glance will serve to reveal that they are precisely what they profess to be, that is, an account of how the author, an eager secular scholar dedicated to the discovery of "truth," took in turn the many experimental paths traced by honored older teachers and philosophers. Finding them ultimately all to be blind alleys, he was at long last induced to try the path of Christ, thereby arriving happily not only at the truth he had for years been searching for in vain but also at the ineffably joyful assurance of his union with God, maker of heaven and earth and of the total creature world. In the light of the confessor's constantly repeated avowal this conclusion of his search must be regarded as the theme and substance of his book. Indeed, it is his intense concentration on his theme that has made the *Confessions* a work of Christian guidance which ever since its publication has inspired countless readers to cherish it as a source of divine enlightenment supplementary to and hardly inferior to the Bible.

The *Confessions* therefore meets the first requirement of abiding literature, whether secular or religious: it has a theme. The theme is announced at once by the giving over of the first four pages to a helplessly stammering praise of God. Only after this irrepressible explosion does the convert launch on his birth with the disclosure of the few facts already recounted. So uncontrollable is his joy over his reformed state of being that each item of his infant development—the milk of the breast, the first flinging about of limbs and voice—is attended by a fresh outburst of thanks to his new-found God. This alternation of biographical items and magnification of the Lord is so outstanding a compositional feature of the *Confessions* that its form might not inappropriately be described as a dialogue between the blissful Christian convert and his God. St. Augustine himself suggests the dialogue idea as determining the structure of his book by describing it in a later work in the following terms: "The thirteen books of my 'Confessions' praise God, holy and good, on occasion of that which has in me been good or evil."[1]

We have already noted that St. Augustine on looking back from his newly attained Christian altitude on his acts of youthful misbehavior condemned them as undoubtedly evil. But these boyhood evils were as nothing compared with the evils which, by his own report, descended upon him when, beginning with his university studies, he sought among the current philosophies and faiths the one unmistakably stamped with the seal of truth. Let us recall in this connection that to him and to his pagan contemporaries in general truth was not, as in most present-day philosophies, a continuing and cumulative revelation but an unchanging absolute hidden behind the fleeting phenomena that beguile our fragile senses. In essence the *Confessions* is a report on this tireless search for the ultimate verity. It absorbed St. Augustine completely from his nineteenth to his thirty-third year, when, after ceaseless painful doubts, he found what he had been seeking by falling elatedly at the feet of

1. See Preface, xv, which quotes from the *De dono perseverantiae*.

Christ. This perturbed fourteen-year period is divided into two distinct sections which call for separate characterization. The first section, which embraces the by far larger number of years, carried him, after unbroken intellectual travail, to the startling revelation that only the Christian system of thought revealed the fixed goal of his endeavor, the unchanging, the eternal God. But an unreasoning, stubborn resistance kept him from submitting to the prescribed crowning act of conversion and caused him to put off for a few more years, constituting the second stage of his conversion process, the termination of his inner conflict by accepting the indispensable requirement of baptism.

The most interesting chapter of St. Augustine's extended, painful search for truth among the available philosophies and faiths of the age involves his association with the Manicheans. The originator of this cult was a Persian, Mani by name, who compounded his system of an agglomeration of Persian, Greek, and other haphazard elements. Quite possibly its very electicism was the source of its attraction for the young scholar seeking enlightenment by following every available avenue of thought. Although he never formally joined the Manicheans, for some years he identified himself with the group, in spite of certain fantastic superstitions they entertained that offended his intelligence. The inevitable break was delayed until the twenty-ninth year of his life and befell in connection with a visit to Carthage of a certain Faustus, celebrated as the leading propounder of the Manichean faith. St. Augustine was promised by his fellow believers, and confidently expected, a resolution of his accumulated doubts by this inspired spokesman of the sect. When he discovered that the great man could not satisfy a single one of his many scruples, he was filled with such disgust that he abruptly abandoned the group that had so long held him in thrall.

Simultaneously with this act of liberation he reached the happy assurance that only Christianity could satisfy his obsessive intellectual preoccupation, which was, as we are aware and may never forget, the unchanging God, sole guarantor of an unchanging, timeless truth. Deeply persuaded though he now was that he had arrived at the goal of his long intellectual search, he found himself facing an obstacle of a non-intellectual and peculiarly personal sort. This was his inability to bring himself to take the final step into the Christian fold by breaking with his long-established sexual habits. St. Augustine had a completely honest mind which he revealed in the long inner debate recorded by him over this crucial issue. Steeped from boyhood in the loose pagan morality, he had from puberty indulged himself in the fornication against which his Christian mother never ceased to warn him and which led him, on reaching the years of maturity, to set up his household with a succession of concubines. It is easy to agree that with his vigorous body and lust of life he would be moved to cling to this practice long after he had become convinced that it would have to be totally renounced before he could present himself for baptism. The fierce character of the new crisis is demonstrated by its requiring a three years' struggle on his part to overcome it. He does not mince words in laying his quandary before his readers. Long after he had disciplined himself to accept the orthodox Christian doctrine that the daughters of Eve are the temptresses and taproot of all evil, he could not bring himself to break with the need, according to his own frank avowal, of being "folded in female arms."

While continuing in this last preconversion phase to earn his livelihood as a professor of rhetoric, he was pressed to seek relief from prolonged inner suffering by a change of residence. He abandoned Africa to go first to Rome and, after a short stay in the declining world capital, to move thence to Milan, which at the time had risen to an equal level of importance. Here his destiny fulfilled itself. He fell under the influence of the bishop of Milan, St. Ambrose, the leading Christian figure of his day; but even so his conversion continued to be delayed because of his inability once and for all to conquer the lust of the flesh. A factor in his hesitation, which he reveals only indirectly but which in this writer's view fell heavily into the scales, was that, owing to his lifelong pursuit of knowledge by the dialectical method, he expected to be swept across the last barrier to conversion by the force of purely intellectual argument. Although it would be an error to deny that analytical thought has sometimes played a role in the phenomenon of conversion, in order to make it the soul-shaking experience it has been in the case of the famous converts of history, it has to take place in the emotional depths lying unmeasured fathoms below the level of consciousness.

Therewith we come to what we may call the emotional leap by which St. Augustine cleared the last obstacle to his conversion. The story constitutes the climax of his book and discloses how reason, hitherto the mainstay of his being, broke down before a miracle. It matters not a pin's weight that in the view of confirmed rationalists the miracle he records will never be regarded as other than pure self-delusion. To the overcharged mind of the shaken St. Augustine, heaven itself made a sign when, sitting one day weeping in his garden, he heard a child intone monotonously again and again: "Take up and read, take up and read." When the words at last penetrated his inattention, he proceeded as in a trance to the volume of the Apostle Paul he had been poring over and, opening it at random, laid his finger on the text: "Put ye on the Lord Jesus Christ and make no provision for the flesh." With these words all doubts vanished as by magic, the gates of heaven swung wide open, and he hurried with the good news to the patiently enduring Monica, who, he says, and we can readily believe, "leaped for joy."

With undaunted resolution he now cleansed his household of its turpitude, broke his last tie with the pagan world of thought by abandoning his rhetoric professorship, and, together with his devoted companion, Alypius, who like himself hailed from Africa, retired to a villa in the neighborhood of Milan to receive the prescribed instruction preparatory to baptism. By this crowning act, conducted by the saintly Bishop Ambrose in person, the two friends were at Easter of the the year 387 solemnly received into the church. We note with a start that a gifted fifteen-year-old son of St. Augustine, now mentioned for the first time, was included in the ceremony. Peace of mind achieved, St. Augustine had no reason for further delaying his return to Carthage. The Mediterranean crossing was effected via Ostia, the port of Rome, and there occurred the death of Monica, who had had the unspeakable happiness of seeing her prayers on behalf of her erring son at last answered. St. Augustine

repaid her for her unwavering faith with a loving account
of her life, which is one of the memorable passages of his
book.

With the baptism achieved, the theme of the *Confessions*
had been brought to its close; and if St. Augustine, besides
being an instinctive searcher for truth, had also been an instinctive artist, he would have laid down his pen at this
point. However, to the nine books he required to round off
his central theme, he added four more, which do not bear
on it in any discernible way. They are therefore, artistically
considered, a superfluity and a blot. It matters not that for
religious-minded readers the substance of these four books
of sheer supererogation may have considerable interest; the
fact remains that they lack relevance to the conversion
theme treated in the nine preceding books. In support of
what might otherwise be thought an unsubstantiated charge,
let us have a look at these superfluous appendages. Book x,
while following—and definitely not for the first and only
time in the *Confessions*—an exceedingly rambling course,
treats of the role of memory in our lives and of the importance at all times of a habitual personal continency.
Book xi, veering sharply from such prevailingly ethical dis-
cussions, turns to the Old Testament and plumbs the theological implications of its solemn opening declaration: "In
the beginning God created the heaven and the earth." With
what affects at least the average secular reader as intolerable
verbal contortionism, Books xii and xiii continue to probe
into this majestic affirmation until it is found to anticipate
all the essential elements of Christian orthodoxy as developed by the post-Pauline theologians. It may safely be
wagered that nine out of every ten readers of the *Confessions*

43

will refuse to read on after the ninth book, revealing by that decision that in their opinion the author has overshot the mark and, unrestrained by the inner check of the born artist, lost himself in dark theological byways.

It must be admitted that St. Augustine, exclusively concerned as long as he lived with the problem of God, in all probability gave not the slightest thought to the aesthetic issue involved in composition and that he would have met the charge of his offense against literary form with unmoved equanimity. But as, in accordance with our declaration at the beginning, we are judging his two works containing secular matter by established secular criteria, we cannot dispense ourselves from noting his shortcomings, whether in the matter of form or in the related matter of style. The English translator of the Latin original tells us in his Preface that his aim was to achieve "the greatest clearness with the greatest faithfulness." The present writer suspects that he achieved an excessive faithfulness and that, while by this practice he caught some of the stateliness inherent in a monumental language like Latin, he also weighted his text with a good deal of awkwardness and involution. A version concerned primarily with intelligibility would doubtless greatly promote circulation. Admittedly what is here indicated as a shortcoming of the translator cannot be attributed to St. Augustine. What stems from him alone and is the outstanding structural feature of the book is the almost uninterrupted praise of God. Although it will be conceded without debate that praise of God is more uplifting when sounded by poetry than by prose, it is conceivable that a prose as charged with sincerity as that of St. Augustine might almost as surely have touched the heart as verse. But this is not actually the case, and for a reason unmistakably deriving from St. Augustine's lifelong immersion in dialetical argument. True, in order to overleap the last obstacle to conversion, he triumphantly threw off his dialectical harness; but, on proceeding to write his *Confessions,* he again dropped back to his habitual syllogistic manner. Without abating his new-found religious conviction, he resumed his settled practice of reviewing the presumptive attributes of an unchanging God and could never finish with exalting his power, his goodness, his mercy, his majesty. Everyone lending a willing ear to St. Augustine's rhetoric will bow to its special quality of mixed humility and exultation; but no secular ear will, after the tenth or fifteenth repetition of this unvarying litany, fail to become surfeited to the point of revulsion and to cry out against its excess. That St. Augustine himself never wearied of his prosy ecstasy is proof of his single-minded religious focus and serves to confirm that he lacked the artist's instinct to avoid repetition and be governed by considerations of balance and proportion.

Even with this defect ascribable to his concentrated religious faith, his incessant praise of God might have escaped the depressing decline to tedium, if he could, at least occasionally, have freed himself from his intellectual chains and given himself to the swift, irrational torrent to which he owed his immediate view of God and his miraculous conversion. Then, conceivably at least, he would have resorted to one of the two vehicles alone adequate to the divine theme —poetry and music. Innumerable are the instances showing that solely to these two vehicles is granted the supreme expression of God's unfathomed mystery. When Dante in his ascent to paradise approached its blinding summit, St. Bernard sounded the hymn to Mary beginning "Virgine madre, figlia del tuo figlio," which confounds all intelligence in pure emotion; and when in his *Messiah* Handel reached his culminating praise of God, he found no recourse other than to let his chorus of men and women, symbolic of the entire creature world, sing out a cluster of meaningless, ecstatic syllables.

The intellect-bound St. Augustine could not take wing with Dante to the seat of heaven or with Handel have all the nations of the earth join in a rhapsodic Hallelujah.

With the *City of God* we enter on a vastly enlarged religious world. The *Confessions* is a story of strictly personal scope composed with a view to easing the passage into the Christian fold of the many hesitating pagan contemporaries of St. Augustine. The *City of God,* on the other hand, proposes nothing less than to replace the dying pagan world with a new and radically different world shaped by views of the relation between God and man derived from the sacred writings incorporated in the Bible. It required an event that rocked the foundations of society to move St. Augustine to raise himself to the role of herald of an entirely new social and religious order. That event was the capture of the ancient capitol of the Roman Empire by a horde of invading barbarians.

On returning to Africa after his conversion, St. Augustine entered the ministry of the Catholic church and, because of his exceptional mental vigor and tireless activity in the church's service, had by the year A.D. 395 been elevated to the bishopric of Hippo (now the insignificant French African port of Bona). By that time he was already regarded as what he has ever since been held to be—the leading ecclesiastical figure of the Latin West. Meanwhile the threat represented by the German tribes camped along the borders of the Roman Empire had become steadily more ominous. After repeated penetrations of Italy, Alaric, king of the West Goths, in the year 410 reached Rome and captured it, following a weak resistance. Unable to keep it firmly in his grasp, he abandoned it after a cruel looting. The momentous event struck the contemporary world, persuaded of the eternity of Rome, as starkly unbelievable; and since it happened within a generation of the establishment in A.D. 382 of Christianity as the only permissible form of public worship, it produced a powerful resurgence of the outlawed paganism. The adherents of the proscribed faith ventured once more into the open, vehemently asserting that the fall of Rome had taken place because of the rejection of the ancient gods who had presided protectively over the city's birth and to whom was due its long-continued pre-Christian ascendancy.

The outcry was general and massive enough profoundly to shake Christian confidence. Alarmed by this turn, the never wavering Bishop of Hippo undertook to reassure his fellow believers with the arguments on behalf of the new faith wherewith his heart and mind perpetually overflowed. It will be recalled that his first decisive turning to Christianity occurred when he became persuaded that it alone among the contending faiths of the age rested on the one eternal God and that the irrefragable evidence of his eternity was supplied by the writings embraced within the Christian canon. He thus became the author of a book beside which all other books dealing with religion were as ropes of sand. It characterizes the completeness of the conversion he had achieved that he no longer regarded the truth of the book of his devotion as subject to question in any respect. It was truth absolute. His important supplementary position, the direct opposite of his earlier rationalist outlook, was: believe first and intellectual enlightenment will follow as a matter of course; or, as he put it in his native Latin, *immo crede ut intelligas.* In this uncompromising state of mind he undertook to stop the mouths of the blasphemers of Christianity and in the year 413 began the work on which, with frequent long intermissions due to the absorbing demands on him of his episcopal office, he labored until 426, that is, for thirteen years.

A work that it took thirteen years to finish was certain to follow a wavering line of development and to pick up much matter alien to its original intention. Overlooking numerous minor deviations, we encounter a definite structural break and an admittedly fresh start when the author, having disposed of the pagan calumnies touching the capture of Rome, hit upon the striking and original concept that the world he lived in was divided between the two unorganzied and invisible societies of the godly and the ungodly or, as he chose to put it, between the sons and daughters of heaven and the sons and daughters of earth. Furthermore, he went on to say, far from being of recent origin, these two opposed societies had led their separate existences from the beginning of history. Nor was their remote birth a matter of conjecture. Considering first the heavenly society, he declared its story was unfolded in the most venerable religious document of the Western world, in the Old Testament, where after more than fifteen hundred years it reached its foretold culmination with the coming of Christ on the blessed mission commemorated in the New Testament. This heavenly group was always a minority society compared with the much more numerous earthly society, of which there was equally early but less authoritative evidence in the accredited settlements along the Nile and Tigris-Euphrates valleys. Beginning with this manifestly lower social group in the fertile bottom lands of the Near Eastern river systems, this earthly society gradually spread over the whole Mediterranean basin, culminating after many war-crowded centuries in the victorious, all-embracing empire of Rome.

St. Augustine had filled ten divisions, called "books," with his original defense theme of Christianity before he launched on his second and far more significant theme of the two contrasted societies of good and evil. To this he then devoted the twelve remaining books of the total work. From the time of the Greeks a society organized into what we moderns would call a state was commonly designated a city (*civitas*), for the simple reason that the earliest form of a tightly organized community sprang from the fusion effected among small interdependent urban groups. It followed that, although the twelve concluding books concerned themselves equally with the two opposed societies which the ruling usage named cities, so much greater emphasis inescapably fell on the divinely oriented city that the completed work took its title from this preference and has come down the ages as the *Civitas Dei,* the "City of God."

The first printed edition of the Latin original of the *City of God* was issued at Basel in 1522 with an introduction by Erasmus, the foremost scholar of the age. A century later, in 1610 to be exact, it received its first English rendering by John Heeley. Possessed of the sonorous style, apparently the birthright of all writers of the Elizabethan period, Heeley contrived a version nobly inspired but too intricate and grammatically involved for the taste of our day. However, much of the admitted difficulty of his translation is attributable to St. Augustine himself, who loved to draw out his arguments to an inordinate length and also delighted in the rhetorical devices of the Hellenistic culture wherein he had been immersed from his youth. These tendencies induced a regrettable loquacity which caused his Latin original to be spun out to twelve hundred pages, and the familiar English two-volume "Everyman's" edition runs to seven hundred and fifty pages, in spite of numerous welcome cuts. Much more drastic cuts would, in this writer's opinion, be justified, since, in addition to the frequent repetitions necessitated by the interrupted manner of the composition, St. Augustine inclined, contrary to the practice of the best writers in every tongue and age, to an excessive fulness of statement.

The ten-book first section of the *City of God,* which owed its origin to St. Augustine's passionate urge to defend Christianity in the controversy over the fall of Rome, invites attention as affording us our earliest opportunity to become acquainted with the idiosyncrasies of his argumentative procedure. Let us begin with Book i and note the unflagging energy with which St. Augustine refutes the pagan charge that the calamities suffered by Rome through Alaric's capture were to be imputed to the newly adopted religion of Christ. Presently he broadens the discussion by taking up the bloody and ruthless action of conquerors throughout the ages and then lets himself be diverted to such not even remotely cognate matters as the burial of the saints, the non-effect of the degradation through rape of holy virgins, the sharp opposition of Christian teaching to the pagan practice of suicide. While it is impossible to trace a logical line of development in this capricious heaping of subject matter, it does undoubtedly throw light on the clear-cut distinction between what to St. Augustine was the vile and corrupt world of the perishing Roman Empire and the cleansed and righteously directed world of Christianity, which was irresistibly replacing it.

We encounter an identical procedure in the remaining nine books of this first section. Book ii, for example, starts out with reminding the readers of the many miseries the Romans endured during the regime of their ancient gods, whereupon, without explanation or apology, he turns aside to discuss such evil Roman practices as marriage by capture (the rape of the Sabine women), the mass murders of the dictator Sulla, the systematic subversion of public morals by scurrilous plays. The raw facts are floated, on the one hand, on the same undercurrent of savage disgust with every aspect of Roman society as in Book i and, on the other hand, on an unbounded enthusiasm for the emergent nobler world of Christianity. And the following eight books repeat this morally inspired but illogical procedure with ever fresh instances of the total incompatibility between the older pagan and the newer Christian society. Then, with apparent suddenness but really because of the gradual ripening and consolidation of his thought, he arrives with the close of Book x at the second theme of his work, the coexistence from the beginning of time of the two actual but unorganized societies of the children of heaven and the children of earth.

To make certain that his readers shall not miss his change

of plan, he opens Book xi with this express announcement: "I set pen to paper, intending first to show the beginning of these two cities." And what is the source or the main source of a knowledge so remote and recondite that no one before him had ever claimed its possession? Simply the canonical Scriptures, which, stemming as he believed from God himself, contain the everlasting truth that is beyond challenge and demands unqualified acceptance by an act of faith. Commanding this infallible guide, he is able to propound the origin and development of the two cities with an unshaken assurance. Accordingly he relates the Bible story of creation, of Adam and Eve, their sin and expulsion from paradise, and their subsequent life of sorrow on earth, until he arrives at their sons, Cain and Abel. These two he offers as the ancestors, respectively, of the two divergent cities— Cain, the murderer, of the city of earth; the slain Abel, of the heavenly city. To follow Abel's line of descent onward to Noah and thence to Abraham, to David, to Christ, is a historical tour de force unequaled before or since and made possible only by a fanatic faith supplemented by the mental gymnastics of a master-dialectician.

The lively details assembled in order to bring to life Abraham, Isaac, Jacob, Moses, and the other protagonists of the saga of the heavenly city cast a veil of deceptive verisimilitude over an otherwise painfully wilful construct. On taking up the parallel development of the far less significant society of the children of earth, a procedure is adopted so hurried and unsubstantial as to create nothing better than a blur. Instead of enumerating the many warring primitive groups of the Near Eastern river systems and the adjoining Mediterranean basin, our impatient historian is content to proceed selectively and to present Assyria and Rome as the outstanding predatory and plainly evil creations of the area and to concede to Rome the distinction of having terminated the centuries-long ferocious conflicts among them by subjecting all their peoples to its universal empire. The historically numerous cities of earth and evil were at last merged into a single city.

It must be clearly understood that St. Augustine's two hypothetical societies should not be identified with the two actual societies of his time—the church and the Empire—although a certain inner relationship between them may not be denied. It was fundamental with him that his two societies had no visible organization and that their membership freely crossed existing organizational and language lines. Therefore, while the church of his time was in his view undoubtedly constituted in large measure of individuals belonging to the heavenly city, he held that it might also include elements which, comparable to wolves in sheeps' clothing, had joined the church for the purely selfish reason of security and prestige. And, again, while admittedly the Empire embraced in the main the devotees of the earthly city, it might conceivably include individuals who by their actual conduct and spiritual outlook could fairly be reckoned members of the heavenly city. At great pains to define the constitutive principle of each of his two opposed realms with the greatest clarity, St. Augustine frequently returned to this crucial point. In his most illuminating statement he offered the following distinction between them: "Two loves have given origin to these two cities, self-love in contempt of God unto the earthly city, love of God in contempt of self to the heavenly city."

It will not have escaped the informed reader that the two cities of St. Augustine, both in existence from the beginning of time, are not in accord with strict Christian orthodoxy. Orthodox doctrine represented Adam and Eve as the parents of the human race, who by their disobedience had brought everlasting punishment on all their descendants. The common teaching took no account of celestially directed individuals who by continuing to follow the call of the Lord constituted the invisible and presumably saved company of St. Augustine's City of God. Strict orthodoxy further decreed damnation as the universal lot until such time as God should take pity and cancel the sin of Adam and Eve by the mission and sacrifice of his beloved son. While St. Augustine does not openly quarrel with this narrow orthodox view of salvation, he decidedly extended its range by admitting to the rewards of heaven a company, no matter how small and highly selective, which from mankind's beginning had kept the faith and constituted the invisible City of God. This is so important as to be central for the understanding of St. Augustine's theological position. It shows how St. Augustine found God, the universal Father, by pagan dialectic reasoning before he found him by an act of faith in Christianity.

The two cities were as widely apart in origin as they were widely apart in their predestined respective goals. The heavenly city of this world was represented as a foreshadowing of the actual heavenly city of the saints and angels reigning in the supersensuous world, and it was held out to the faithful in Christ as their reward on their demise together with the blessing of the "Supreme Good." About the nature of this culminating felicity there was not the faintest wavering of a doubt; "Supreme Good" was peace everlasting joined

to everlasting life with God. By a parallel logic the punishment which on their demise awaited the members of the
earthly city was everlasting torment under Satan, ruler of
the torture chambers of the eternal world of hell. There
were no great sinners and little sinners according to St.
Augustine. Purgatory was established for the less culpable
group by later Catholic teaching whereby this category was
enabled to expiate its less than mortal sins and hope ultimately to reach paradise. St. Augustine, like all logicians,
was a Rhadamanthine judge in whose view the verdict pro-
nounced on the departing soul was invariably either heaven
or hell with no middle ground between.

Let it be confessed that could St. Augustine be confronted
with our exposition of the origin of the two cities together
with their respective goals he would be moved sadly to shake
his head. He would declare it, and very properly, to be over-
simplified and then would indicate, with the usual wounded
author's pride, that the leading features of his argument
which are here fused into a close, intelligible statement are
scattered in the original over widely separated sections of his
work without a clearly indicated connection among them.
Frankly admitting both charges, this writer nonetheless ventures to submit that he has performed a distinct editorial
service in reducing the swollen tide of the saint's widely scattered divagations on his two fabled cities to their manage-
able essence. In the *City of God* as in the *Confessions* St.
Augustine's defective artistry is noticeable. While his energy
in setting forth his belief in the two societies and in assembling from history, the Bible, and his own experience the
evidence calculated to substantiate his theory arouses admiration, his painful inability to impress on his exposition

an indispensable unity and order forever deprives the *City of God* of the character of a work of art.

This stricture on his book would not have offended the saint himself, since never for even a fleeting moment did he conceive of himself as engaged in producing a work of art. Intent only on his theme of the heavenly and the satanic city, he brought his immense labors to a close with a commingled humility and dignity which is so perfect a disclosure of his mind and heart that it is a pleasure to set it down: "I think I have discharged the debt of this great work with the help of God. Let those who think I have done too little, and those who think I have done too much, grant me a favorable pardon. But let those who think I have done enough, accepting it with a kind congratulation, give no thanks unto me but unto the Lord with me. Amen."

It should not diminish by a measurable shade the noble humility of these concluding words for the writer to append a conclusion of his own, imposed by the very different world view of the twentieth century. Our exposition has shown that the *City of God* cannot be accommodated to any present-day definition of history and that, by current understanding, it falls not under the head of history at all but under that of theology and philosophy. It follows that since history conceived as a branch of literature is the common bond among the authors examined in the studies brought together in the present volume St. Augustine should not have been associated with them. The writer's reason for doing so—his excellent reason as he thinks—is that for eight hundred years after the appearance of the *City of God* it was regarded not only as history but as the only history worthy of attention and that it shaped the outlook of Western mankind throughout that period. Not the least remarkable feat of the deep Middle Ages is that theology should have overshadowed, nay, blotted out for eight long centuries, what is commonly conceived as history.

Great as was the shock St. Augustine experienced on the capture of Rome in 410, the event proved no more than a curtain raiser to the vast socio-political convulsion that followed. Before the fifth century had run its course, the component provinces of Rome had each in turn been seized and settled by one or another of the conquering German tribes, and the ancient Roman Empire throughout its western half had been brought to an ignominious end. St. Augustine's *City of God* was finished in 426. Only a few years later one of the most enterprising of the invading German peoples, the Vandals, reached Africa after crossing the Mediterranean at Gibraltar. Their plan was to set up a Vandal kingdom in this rich and as yet unplundered province. In the year 430 they laid siege to St. Augustine's episcopal seat of Hippo. Details are lacking, but we know that the greatest Christian figure of the West died during the progress of the siege.

If appearances were the true measure of events it might be concluded that with the overrunning of western Europe by the German tribes the life-work of St. Augustine had been destroyed. This proved to have been far from the case for the single reason that the Roman Catholic church, to which he had imparted a confident fresh vigor, lived on with undiminished vitality after the destruction of the Roman state. Uplifted by its brightly glowing faith, it undertook the gigantic task of converting to Christianity the heathen conquerors within its embrace. In this purpose, which called for self-sacrificing missionary labors nobly sustained through generations, it achieved a sweeping triumph. On abandoning their rude native cults, the converted invaders, with an exemplary submissiveness, accepted the guidance of the church and the far-shining emblem of its unity and power, the Roman pope. In this manner there slowly unrolled the centuries of Western civilization we commonly call the "Middle Ages" whose summary expression may be said to have been a continuing social and political barbarousness gradually mitigated by a Christianity of a steadily tightened organization and a widened spiritual authority. In the long-continuing cultural barbarousness of the period and in the gradual deepening of its Christian substance, St. Augustine had a notable part.

First, as to his at least partial responsibility for the low cultural level of the early Middle Ages. We have learned that, up to the time of his conversion at the age of thirty-three, St. Augustine pointed his studies exclusively and passionately to the mastery of the Greco-Roman heritage of philosophy and letters. At the time of his conversion he was without question the outstanding living embodiment of the traditional classical culture. But when he became a Christian, he began to attack, with the immense energy of his nature, the corruptions of the decaying Roman society, more specifically, its hideous idolatrous polytheism, its lewd theatrical and cruel, bloody gladiatorial spectacles, and its dissolute private manners, particularly exemplified in the loose relation of the sexes. He was moved to lay the ax indiscriminately to the pagan past in order to beat it into indistinguishable ruin. We can but believe that he must at times have felt a strong prompting to spare some of his beloved studies

58

and particularly the dialectical procedure that served as the methodological foundation of the whole classical superstructure. Be that as it may, the effect of the uncompromising war he felt obliged to wage against the pagan past was to discredit its every phase and feature.

Inescapably there followed a dimming of the intellectual skies to an all but total darkness, a condition which, unrelieved for centuries, was not terminated until the coming of the phase of Western civilization commonly called the Renaissance. The word means "rebirth," and the rebirth the Renaissance celebrates was substantially the recovery and reabsorption of the scorned and discarded classical learning. In this manner there was inaugurated, beginning with the fourteenth century and effective throughout the Christian West, a new period of an increasingly free intellectual inquiry that continues into the modern age.

Immeasurably more important in the deep perspective of the centuries than St. Augustine's assistance in extinguishing the faint intellectual light still asparkle in the dissolving pagan world was his share in endowing the surviving Christian society with what has proved to be its central as well as its most vital and enduring element. This was the teaching of the universal Fatherhood of God. It should never be forgotten that, as he tells us in the *Confessions,* his conversion to Christianity began with his reaching the conviction that the Christian God was the unchanging, the eternal God, sole creator of heaven and earth. According to this all-embracing doctrine not only did the members of the Christian church lie under God's governing hand but so did all peoples inhabiting the continents and islands of our far-flung earth. One and all—believers and non-believers, the white, the

black, the yellow people, and all the mixtures of these colors
—were alike God's children. Whether living as individuals
in deserts or assembled in loose groups or consolidated states,
they formed a common human brotherhood under a universal Father.

This is the particular intellectual and emotional doctrine
which St. Augustine wove masterfully and indestructibly
into the unfolding Christianity of his day. It is the forever lamentable fact that his great teaching, while never ceasing
to be invoked, has been savagely flouted and trampled under
foot in the uninterrupted conflicts that have been the unhappy lot of man on earth. Nevertheless, the central truth it
embodies has never ceased to shine as an unextinguished
beacon above the murk and roar of history. Following each
new catastrophe in the endless succession of catastrophes that
make up the story of mankind, it has regularly reappeared
above the wreckage, visible usually by no more than a nu-
cleus of undespairing souls moved to blazon forth the Au-
gustinian teaching of universal brotherhood. Never more
than now is it needed as a rallying point against the crass
materialism and godless cynicism that threaten a blackout
of civilization as sweeping as that of the fifth century and,
like it, attended by another indefinitely prolonged medieval
night.

BIBLIOGRAPHICAL NOTE

The *Opera omnia* of St. Augustine were published by J. P.
Migne at Paris, 1841–77; *S. Aurelii Augustini Confessiones,* ed.
Bruder (Leipzig, 1898). There are many English translations of
the *Confessions.* First English version of *De civitate Dei* is by
John Heeley in 1610. There is also a modernized translation.

NICCOLÒ MACHIAVELLI

Political Philosopher

Whatever his genius and literary purpose—and their definition is the aim of this essay—Machiavelli was not a historian. His exclusion from this professional group might as well be established at once as a helpful guide in the proposed portraiture. The outstanding and never failing trait of the individual designated from birth for this craft is an unshaken and unshakable respect for the innumerable small items or facts making up the socio-political stream, the agreed objective of all historical inquiry. Of this instinctive respect Machiavelli had not so much as a trace, with the result that what he offers as history is largely a free invention lacking a solid and indispensable substructure of tested events and, consequently, irritating, annoying, and meaningless.

It will suffice to examine his best-known work of this kind, his *History of Florence,* to justify this unqualified rejection. The first section (Book I) of the work considers Italy from the fall of the Roman Empire to the year 1434. At once it becomes plain that the author's purpose was limited to telescoping the immense happenings of a thousand-year period into a hurried survey offered as a curtain raiser to the usurpation of the Medici, which befell in the survey's terminal year. One of Machiavelli's earliest successors in the field of Florentine history, Ammirato by name, so scorchingly disclosed his predecessor's factual unreliability that one wonders that the work survived the blazing torch Ammirato applied to it. This sixteenth-century Florentine historiographer unhesitatingly asserts that Machiavelli at his pleasure "changed dates, altered names, reshaped the facts, added, took away, diminished," in short, altered the material according to whatever his ruling purpose dictated. No writer since has come to the rescue of Machiavelli's facts.

In addition to proved and trustworthy data historians—as well as enlightened readers, for that matter—of the post-Ammirato centuries have demanded an intelligible world view as a general background to Florentine or any other body of socio-political developments. This Machiavelli so completely fails to supply that he discloses not even a remote awareness that the centuries he covered in his first section incubated a new civilization. With what, in an intelligence as lively as his, one is tempted to ascribe to a simulated stupidity, Machiavelli recounts such capital events as the coronation of Charlemagne at Rome in the year 800, the ecclesiastical reforms of Pope Gregory VII, and the long tug of war between the Emperor Frederick Barbarossa and the Lombard communes in so slack and confused a manner that they do not compose into even a semblance of philosophical meaning. An early suspicion on the part of the reader crystallizes quickly into the conviction that Machiavelli's sense of cultural change was of so dull and unresponsive an order that, in spite of the close concern with the Middle Ages imposed on him by his introductory section, he never realized that he was confronted with that rarest and most startling of phenomena, the birth of a culture—a lapse we may red-letter as the unapproached summit of historical unawareness.

Indubitably, on coming to the domestic history of the Florentine commonwealth there is an improvement. In this area there arose the issue of the conflict for power among groups and parties of the population; that is, the narrator was confronted with a political struggle with the nature of which he had become thoroughly familiar during his fourteen years of service to the post-Medicean republic. This employment will later receive the full treatment it requires, since it became the pivotal episode of his life. At this point let it serve to explain why the dull pace of the *History of Florence* was happily quickened when the experienced officeholder undertook to set forth the local party struggle of which he possessed a firsthand knowledge. But even in this department his roll call of names and the desirable precise profiling of events are unconscionably slurred. In short, while Machiavelli revealed himself in the strictly domestic section of his book as a writer fully at home among the local political rivalries, he does not by a hair's breadth increase our respect for him as a historian.

It may be permitted to examine another and definitely minor work of Machiavelli's in order conclusively to establish our argument of his estrangement from history. Relatively late in life, in the year 1520, he had occasion to visit the neighboring city of Lucca, which two hundred years before Machiavelli's time had risen to a brief Tuscan supremacy under an extraordinarily bold and resourceful military adventurer, Castruccio Castracane by name. Villani and the other Florentine chroniclers contemporary with Castruccio had given full play to his career, which for a brief period hung a black pall over their native city. On arriving at Lucca, Machiavelli discovered that Castruccio, the unique military hero of the Lucchese commune, was still the talk of the town and had recently even been honored by having the story of his life recounted by a patriotic biographer. Any historian worth his salt would have visited Castruccio on arriving at Lucca and, by a critical study of the surviving evidence, have arrived at as clear a picture as possible of the actual role and character of the man. Not so Machiavelli. The real, the historical Castruccio failed to elicit the slightest interest on Machiavelli's part because of his obsession with the dream of an Italian military leader (projected under the title "The Prince" in his famous work of this name) who would put an end to the national impotence by the forcible merger of the country's numerous petty sovereignties. Something like a precursor of the desired liberator could be read into Castruccio's brilliant but short-lived career, and Machiavelli bent himself to the task of distorting the military successes of the Lucchese tyrant by endowing them with a national significance which they by no stretch of the imagination possessed. In other words, he did what no man dedicated to historical actuality has ever done: he passed up the challenge of faithfully portraying a leading personage of a past age in favor of freely invented episodes which fall upon the historically attuned ear with the annoyance of a child's irrelevant prattle.

In thus eliminating Machiavelli from consideration as a historian, we have had occasion to indicate two interests that were vital to him: his concern with Florentine politics and his passionate hope for the unification of Italy by a military genius. Since these two directives derived from his absorbing experience as a Florentine officeholder, it behooves us to follow his official career closely. He was born in 1469, the son of an unimportant lawyer, who, besides owning a house on the left bank of the Arno, not far from the Ponte Vecchio, owned a small farm to the immediate south of the city, by virtue of which he hovered on the thin outer fringe of the landlord class. Young Niccolò, while following in his father's professional footsteps, hoped for an improvement in his lot by an appointment to government office. Not until the overthrow of the Medici and the re-establishment of the republic in 1494 did the situation take a turn favorable to his expectations and even then not at once. For the next four years, until his martyrdom in May, 1498, Girolamo Savonarola all but monopolized the Florentine scene. A month after Savonarola's inhuman judicial murder, Machiavelli, now twenty-nine years old, was appointed head of the Second Chancery and secretary of the Ten, a committee in charge of war.

These rather high-sounding posts did no more than define him as an administrative official charged with carrying out the policies formulated by his superiors. However, since all the business of the state, both domestic and foreign, passed through his two offices, he acquired an unrivaled command of the diverse issues which agitated the republic. His lynxlike attention to details coupled with his penetrating intelligence promptly won him a consideration far beyond his official assignments and led to his being dispatched on informative diplomatic missions. His continued purely administrative character was indicated by his serving merely as government agent on these occasions and not as full-fledged ambassador. When a treaty was to be signed, a dignitary of a higher rank regularly replaced him. Although he had no particular success in his earliest mission, which befell in the year 1499 and took him to the famous virago, Catherina Sforza, countess of Imola and Forlì, his report on it so decidedly satisfied the government that he was assigned to an endless succession of similar tasks. In the course of his fourteen years of service to the state he was sent five times to France, once to Germany, several times to Milan, and at least once to every other Italian polity that impinged in any way on Florentine interests. But far and away his most important missions were concerned with Cesare Borgia during the brief period, from 1500 to 1503, when Cesare's star rose over Italy and filled with feelings of terror and fascination every small sovereign of the Romagna and Umbria, the two neighboring provinces Borgia had staked out as his prospective kingdom.

When in the year 1502 the alarm aroused by Cesare Borgia's encroachments on Florentine territory convinced the citizens that they must strengthen the leading official, the gonfalonier, by appointing him for life instead of for the usual scant two months, Machiavelli's importance was greatly enhanced. The man who won the fortified executive office was Piero Soderini. Soderini, an honorable, if commonplace, republican stalwart, had become so impressed with Machiavelli's unequaled grasp of Florentine problems that he fell into the habit of consulting him on all the affairs of state. This enabled Machiavelli to urge a novel military program, which he had long been persuaded was absolutely necessary. Ever since the fourteenth century Florence, like all the other Italian states, had turned to hireling mercenary troops to prosecute its wars. Although the mercenaries had originally exhibited an undeniable efficiency, they had latterly taken to regularly betraying their trust by selling their services, regardless of contract obligations, to the highest bidder. This treacherous system had become malodorous to everyone, but no one had proposed a viable or even a viable-seeming substitute until Machiavelli advocated intrusting the defense of the state to a national militia. So alien had the thought of personal military service become to the Italian people that the Florentine public greeted Machiavelli's proposal with bursts of derisive laughter. However, the secretary stuck to his point and, after gradually winning Gonfalonier Soderini's support, was able to carry the issue to the Grand Council, the democratic core of the republic's constitution.

It required some years of propaganda activity before the Grand Council, in 1506, passed its first hesitant measure. This went no further than to authorize the peacetime training in arms of the country population. So fiercely was the urban population set against the proposed measure that it was, at least for the time being, expressly exempted from its application. Perhaps the innovation might not have passed the Council in even this shorn form if Florence had not been engaged just then in a fresh and supreme effort to resubject rebellious Pisa to its authority. Ever since the French army's passage through Tuscany in 1494, Pisa had been in revolt against Florence and had withstood every attempt once again to reduce it to subjection. By the time of the creation of the national militia, another invasion of Pisa had been undertaken, this time with grimly serious intent. While mercenaries had again to be employed for the strictly professional work of breaching the Pisan walls, it was found that the many small subsidiary services connected with the conduct of a siege could be safely intrusted to the new and still shaky national militia. We may fairly call the new creation Machiavelli's army, not only because he had been its leading sponsor, but also because its control had been assigned to a special committee of nine which he served as secretary and virtual head. The Pisans so stubbornly defended their independence that it was not until June, 1509, that they opened their gates to the enemy and then only because they could no longer sustain the struggle under the wasting starvation to which they had been reduced.

The conquest of Pisa was the greatest achievement of the reconstituted Florentine republic. It may also be called the banner event of Machiavelli's political career, for not only his devoted intimates of the Second Chancery but the whole Florentine population as well had become persuaded that the steadily improving national militia and the whole relentless drive behind the successful Pisan siege stemmed in last analysis from him.

From this height there was a swift descent for both the republic and its tireless secretary. As Machiavelli had long foreseen there was every probability that divided Italy would sooner or later fall victim to either France or Spain, the two great powers which, ever since King Charles VIII's invasion of 1494, had been girding themselves for this conquest. In the very year of the capture of Pisa, Pope Julius II, a passionate but bungling Italian patriot, had evolved a plan for the ejection of both the loathed invaders from Italian soil. He hoped to achieve his purpose by the united action of the Italians themselves, aroused to exert themselves in a common cause by the patriotic cry "Put the barbarians out!" (*Fuori i barbari!*). The movement proved a miserable fiasco because the hopelessly divided Italians refused to give ear to the pope's call; and Julius II, who had initiated his action by taking the field against the French, was reduced before long to the sorry necessity of appealing for help against the French to the only power capable of meeting them on an equal basis, i.e., the Spaniards. Consequently the nobly inspired war for the liberation of Italy took the ludicrous form of a duel between the two great Western powers to determine to which of them should fall the mastery of the peninsula. In April, 1512, a great battle was fought at Ravenna to decide the issue. It was won by the French in the limited sense that they held the field at the close of the day. But they had no profit from their victory. Lack of provisions obliged them to fall back on their base at Milan, and, when the quarreling commanders could not come to an agreement as to their further course, the disheartened army effected a piecemeal retirement from Lombardy, thereby abandoning the peninsula to the Spaniards as their prize.

This turn of the war brought unqualified disaster to the Florentine republic. On having been pressed by Pope Julius to join the national cause, the government had resolved to cling to its traditional alliance with France. Practically alone among Florentines Machiavelli urged that a neutral attitude offered a better chance of survival. But Gonfalonier Soderini, with a solidly French-minded citizenry behind him, rejected neutrality as a form of betrayal unworthy of a statesman and people of loyal principles. Consequently with the Spaniards and their papal allies in unchallenged control, a congress of the victors held at Mantua resolved to put an end to the Gallicly attached republic and dispatched a Spanish army against Florence to carry out the decree. It should cause no surprise that the republic perished as unheroically as it had lived. Its one chance to go down with flags flying rested with Machiavelli's national militia. But when the insufficiently trained and fundamentally recalcitrant peasant army faced the professional Spaniards at Prato, some ten miles from the capital, it scattered in headlong flight at the first enemy onset. Promptly on reception of the news the mild, weak-willed Soderini gave up the game and abandoned the city in such head-over-heels precipitation that he did not pause for breath until he had reached Ragusa on the eastern—and safer—shore of the Adriatic Sea.

A Florentine citizen committee that hurried to Prato to announce the government's surrender humbly accepted every condition imposed by the Spanish commander. After agreeing to pay the military expenses of the victors, it bowed to the crucial demand to readmit the banished Medici to Florentine citizenship. Thereupon there entered Florence in triumph the two still living sons of Lorenzo the Magnificent—first, the gentlemanly and feckless Giuliano and, a few days later, his older brother, Cardinal Giovanni, a man of a considerable range of talents, who had figured prominently in the recent campaign as the personal representative of Pope Julius II. Their arrogant and empty-headed older brother, Piero, who had been ejected from the rule of the city by the revolution of 1494, was, luckily for the family cause, no longer among the living. Ten years before, he had drowned in the swift waters of a south Italian river, when fleeing with the beaten French before the advancing Spaniards, who by their sweeping victory had acquired what turned out to be their earliest permanent foothold in the peninsula. This foothold was the extensive kingdom of Naples, the French claim to which had caused the first penetration of Italy by King Charles VIII, back in 1494.

Since the two brothers entered Florence at the head of mercenary troops their readmission to citizenship promptly took the form of absolute control. A committee of Medicean partisans, of which Cardinal Giovanni was the undisputed, if concealed, head, dismissed the officials of the defeated republic in order to replace them with trusty Miceans. Machiavelli hoped against hope to be retained in office. But when his name was found on a conspiratorial list, though put there without his consent, his last chance of absorption into the new regime flickered out. Shortsighted moralists have ever since seized the occasion to denounce Niccolò as a timeserver and a turncoat. The judgment will not stand with persons of a wider human outlook. Machiavelli, although a convinced republican, regarded it as more important honorably to serve his country than to identify himself with a form of government which had just given conspicuous proof of its inability to survive amid the prevailing Italian turmoil. His most urgent reason for seeking continued employment was his conviction—and a justified conviction it surely was—that he commanded a sum of political experience of the greatest value to the new rulers of Florence and ultimately to Florence itself.

Refused employment, he retired to his small farm on the southern border of the city, resolved, since he was excluded from putting his knowledge to practical use, to do the next best thing and expound it by the written word. Never did a man make a decision of greater consequence to his reputation, for it caused a relatively unimportant local official condemned to an early oblivion by loss of office to leap into a world fame which envelops his name with undiminished splendor to the present day.

For the contemplated literary work Niccolò had in his possession two outwardly distinct but inwardly related bodies of information. On the one hand, there was the immediate practical knowledge attained by his fourteen years of close observation of the behavior of states, both large and small, in peace and war; on the other hand, through prolonged intensive study of the rich history of classical times, more particularly of the history of Rome, he commanded material from which he might extract heaped instances illustrative of the conduct of the governments of bygone days. For many years while still in active service of the state he had filled his leisure hours with written reflections on the socio-political developments of Rome as expounded by the historian Livy, and these reflections he was letting slowly accumulate in his files under the label *Discorsi sopra la prima deca di Tito Livio* ("Discourses on the First Ten Books of Titus Livius," referred to henceforth under the abbreviated title of *Discourses*).

For Machiavelli contemplating authorship there was therefore no lack of fuel on hand. It required but a spark to ignite it, and that spark was supplied by an event of incalculable scope involving the ruling Medici family. In February, 1513, the dynamic, headlong, and blundering Pope Julius II passed from the human scene, and the conclave assembled to name a successor elected Cardinal Giovanni Medici to the highest Christian dignity. Adopting the title Leo X, he set up his residence in the Vatican as custom required. On abandoning Florence, he intrusted the government of the city to his brother Giuliano, whose unfitness for this or any responsible post whatever had not yet been revealed. To an observer on the side lines and therefore also to Machiavelli, the personally attractive Giuliano had become the actual ruler of the city and had the unexampled opportunity of drawing on the vast resources of the papacy to fortify his position. In the eyes of the ex-secretary, thirsting for re-employment in the service of the state, here was a heaven-sent chance to recommend himself to the untried Medici by imparting to him his own invaluable knowledge on the conduct of rulers under the disturbing conditions prevailing in Italy and Europe.

The earliest avowal of his design is recorded in a letter to his friend Francesco Vettori, dated December 10, 1513. Therein he says: "I have composed a little book *De Principatibus* debating what a principate is, what the species are, how they are gained, how they are kept, how they are lost"; and he adds that since his exposition should be instructive especially to a new prince, he was dedicating it to his Magnificence, Giuliano de' Medici. This essay, a first draft, he continued to refine and enlarge for the next few years, in the course of which the incapable Giuliano was replaced as

73

Pope Leo's representative by his and Leo's nephew, son of their older brother Piero. This was Lorenzo, young, vigorous, and ambitious. Accordingly Machiavelli's finished work, provided with the more compact title *Il Principe* ("The Prince"), was not inscribed to the Magnificent Giuliano as originally intended but to the Magnificent Lorenzo.

In the years immediately following its completion in 1516, *The Prince* circulated only in manuscript form and was not available to the general public until it was printed in 1532, five years after its author's death. It then promptly released a clamor of universal abhorrence which the present-day reader, with the illuminating and disillusioning experience of two world wars behind him, finds it difficult to understand but which is completely intelligible in the light of the political theory which ruled opinion in Machiavelli's day. This theory was of medieval and theological origin and concerned itself with enumerating the duties of a ruler unfailingly conceived both as a faithful subject of the church and as a moral exemplar to his people. There was always a chasm, and often a yawning one, between theory and practice, but it did not seem greatly to trouble anybody until Machiavelli, on closely scanning it, was shocked to the depth of his being by its vacuous unreality. His purpose ran to replace the distorted picture drawn by ecclesiastically inspired writers with a description as accurate as possible of the actual behavior of the rulers, not only of his own, but of every age of which records survived. Fundamental to his position was the view that the state was and had ever been an organization primarily concerned with survival and growth and that it had never let its pursuit of these two related ends be hampered by religious and moral scruples.

The goal of the state and its ruler was power, and, while states ought to be and were actually concerned also with the well-being of their subjects, in their relation to one another states were engaged in what could be unqualifiedly described as a naked power struggle.

Let us now turn directly to *The Prince* and, to begin with, agree that it is not a logically ordered, close-knit essay but is composed of distinct sections which by reason of an inner association yet form a literary unit. The first and by far the largest section embraces the first eleven chapters and may with considerable assurance be taken to be the work to which Machiavelli referred in his letter to Vettori of December 10, 1513. In that letter he declared, as already noted, that he had treated the variety of existing principates with special attention to the hazards to which a newly created principate is exposed. For this reader, as for every alerted student of the text, this section reaches its culmination in chapter vii, which is entitled "On the Principates That Are Obtained through the Military Powers of Others and from Fortune." It gives an almost lyrically sustained account of how Cesare Borgia, son of Pope Alexander VI, cut out a state for himself from the territories of the church by means of military action combined with murder, falsehood, trickery, and every known diabolical device. Niccolò approves of every measure adopted by Cesare because it was inexorably required for the fulfilment of the unitary purpose he was pursuing in the midst of the enormously complicated situation which enveloped him.

Let no one for a moment imagine that Machiavelli demeaned himself by glossing over the wickedness of Borgia's acts. Their wickedness was undebatable, but they assumed, in his estimate, an excusable character because they were directed at the replacement of the many petty tyrants of the Romagna and Umbria with a single tyrant whose concern would be the common good of the inhabitants of the immediately appropriated territory and who might be conceived as the forerunner of a tyrant on a national scale who, again for the common good, would forge the many contentious sovereignties of the peninsula into a united Italy.

It is plain that Machiavelli believed that Borgia's abhorrent deeds were justified on the theoretical ground—generally and falsely in later European history attributed to the Jesuits —that the end hallows the means. In which connection let us note that, quite apart from the moral chaos into which this doctrine plunges society, it is far from being the sure road to the success at which it aims. Nor did it prove a sure road in Cesare Borgia's case. Machiavelli is inclined to ascribe the ending of Cesare's early triumphs in ultimate failure to chance or fortune, to which he concedes so large a role in the affairs of men that he devotes a whole later section of his book (chap. xxv) to their capricious action. However, after enthusiastically indorsing every measure of Cesare's as inescapably imposed by his role of a new or usurper prince set on perpetuating his rule, he does permit himself to point out a single possible slip-up of his hero. It occurred when, on the unexpected death of his father, Pope Alexander VI, Cesare permitted the cardinals to raise his deadly enemy, the vigorous Julius II, to the papacy. Then, unwilling to let this judgment stand in an unsoftened form, Machiavelli offers as an explanation of Cesare's admitted dereliction that he lay smitten almost to death by Roman fever at the time that the election of Alexander's successor to the papacy took place.

Since *The Prince* continues to discuss principates through the four chapters immediately following the criminal story of Cesare Borgia, we have added assurance that the eleven chapters composing the first section constitute the original essay announced to Vettori in 1513. If this supposition is accepted, the chapters following chapter xi represent additions which, if no longer concerned with defining the different types of principates, at least treat of matters which are their common concern. Thus chapters xii through xiv discuss mercenary troops and military interests in general; another chapter debates whether fortresses are useful or useless to a prince; another deals with the destruction of the best-laid plans by capricious fortune; and still another (chap. xviii) treats of keeping faith under the title "In What Way Faith Should Be Kept by Princes."

It is this chapter, together with chapter vii, dealing ecstatically with Cesare Borgia, that became the prime movers of the public scandal which *The Prince* on publication so promptly and universally created. The author opens the discussion with a statement morally so impeccable that it might have been lifted from the disquisition on secular government by the orthodox and righteous St. Thomas Aquinas: "Everybody knows how laudable it is in a prince to keep his faith and to be an honest man and not a trickster." This is the idealist position of medieval and ecclesiastical origin; but what is the reality? In sharp contrast to the paper directive we have the iron practice of princes who through the ages act contrary to faith, contrary to humanity, and contrary to religion. From the consequent confusion at the top ruling level it follows that, should a prince be honest (or foolish) enough to consider himself indissolubly bound by the contractual obligations he has assumed, he will inescapably be destroyed by his dishonest neighbors. Our author therefore arrives at the following declaration: "A prudent ruler cannot and should not observe faith when such observance is to his disadvantage." So fully does this position accord with the practice of states throughout the centuries that we would be at a loss to account for the outcry it produced if we did not remind ourselves that Machiavelli's realism precipitated a head-on collision with the ecclesiastically inspired instructions on the conduct of rulers that still dominated the closet thought of the age.

To this writer the material of the chapters supplementary to the first close-knit eleven chapters is so convincingly pertinent to the concerns of a princely ruler that it fuses easily and naturally to the book's core. However, the last chapter (chap. xxvi) poses a problem. The sharp analytical procedure and the cool scientific tone that have obtained up to this point give place to an explosive emotional appeal to Lorenzo, the young ruler of Florence, and to the house of Medici in general to take up the patriotic task of liberating Italy from its tormentors and of securing its independence for all time by unifying its feuding elements under a single scepter. It is incredible that anyone reading this chapter should fail to catch its immediate cry of the heart. Nonetheless there are readers to whom the change of manner has proved so puzzling that they have refused to rate the concluding chapter as other than a hollow rhetorical flourish. To this writer such a judgment stems from the failure to penetrate to Machiavelli's essential nature. While observing

78

in *The Prince* and in all his political writings the scientific detachment by which he might hope to arrive at valid historical conclusions, he was prompted to these studies by a love of country, a love which originally had centered in Florence but which gradually radiated outward from Florence until it embraced all Italy. In one of the last letters he ever wrote, we have the moving avowal: "I love my country more than my soul." From its beginning to its close his life was dominated by this patriotic and even excessively patriotic sentiment. For every sensitive ear the emotional fervor of the closing chapter of *The Prince* is subtly implicit in the whole work. Indeed, as can be read between the lines of the letter to Vettori announcing the new undertaking, it was the patriotic hope aroused by the elevation of Leo X to the papacy that moved him to recommend himself to the Medici by setting forth his unrivaled command of the political problems the restored Medicean principate would have to face.

The sorry mauling *The Prince* received on its appearance was naturally and gleefully extended to its author, who was painted as an authentic son of Satan intent on providing a handbook for tyrants prepared to blot free and Christian governments from the face of the earth. The truth was different and was available in the text itself for every thoughtful reader with an unbiased mind. Undeniably, however, Machiavelli's other political writings are so much more readily revealing as to his true character and opinions that for complete clarification it is indispensable to search them for evidence. These other writings are *History of Florence, Art of War, Discourse on Reforming the Government of Florence,* and the *Discourses on the First Ten Books of Livy.*

Of the *History of Florence* it has already been noted that, while possessing little value as narrative history, it contains a spirited analysis of the political groups which contended for local control. Under no circumstances to be overlooked is the fact that the work reveals no partiality for the Medici, although it was Pope Clement VII who commissioned it, and that from beginning to end the author's attitude is that of an honorable, independent republican without a touch of the satanism with which he was so freely charged by the calumniators and distorters of *The Prince*.

The *Art of War* is an exhaustive discussion bearing on Machiavelli's deep concern with the defense of the state by a home-trained national army instead of by the hireling mercenaries on which his countrymen had come to depend in recent generations. Here, too, we encounter an open mind in search of the truth and ready to follow it to whatever conclusion it leads.

A much richer disclosure of Machiavelli's political mentality is afforded by the *Discourse on Reforming the Government of Florence*. It owed its origin to an invitation issued by Pope Leo X in the year 1519, when the premature death of Lorenzo, the young lord of Florence, produced a most painful crisis. As there was no youthful member of the family available as Lorenzo's successor and as, furthermore, the only two living members of the line were Pope Leo X and his cousin, Cardinal Giulio (afterward Pope Clement VII), both no longer young and pledged as churchmen to celibacy, how to continue the government became a burning issue and how to continue it in Medicean hands an unsolvable riddle. Leo X met the crisis by dispatching Cardinal Giulio to Florence as interim governor. Then, in order to impress his Florentine fellow citizens with a liberal disposition he did not possess, he summoned a number of leading inhabitants to submit written proposals on the best course to be taken in the circumstances. Among those thus honored was Machiavelli, and the document he handed in bore the title *Discourse on Reforming the Government of Florence.* Machiavelli faced a difficulty in his reform proposal which the document reveals on every page. He was a professed republican and believed that a republican government might again be set up, provided the two Medici churchmen could be persuaded to initiate it. In spite of the doubts he must have entertained on this score, he resolved to exhibit an unwavering trust in their patriotic intentions in the hope that his high expectations would somehow lift them to his own moral level. His strict republican faith was manifested in his declaration that the proposed government must commit itself to the common good and avoid favoring any particular citizen group. He represented the Florentine population as composed of three classes—an upper, a middle, and a lowest class—to each of which should be conceded a definite measure of authority. He even advocated the ultimate restoration of the Grand Council of Piero Soderini's period, since it enjoyed general favor as the most democratic institution the city had ever had. In order to simplify the government he advocated the abolition of the numerous existing councils and their replacement by a new central council of sixty-five endowed with complete executive control. The naming of the sixty-five members was to fall to the two Medici princes, who would thus have the honor of inaugurating the government and lending it the invaluable sanction of tradition. And he closed with a note of high-minded encouragement to his two sponsors indicative of his belief that they shared his patriotic intention: "With the government established in this manner, it would not be necessary to make any other provision if your Holiness and the Most Reverend Cardinal were going to live forever. But you have to depart and your wish is to leave a perfect republic supported by all the necessary parties."

Of course nothing came of the project for the reason that the two Medici churchmen were secretly and from the first resolved to perpetuate the rule of their house. To effect this purpose Pope Clement VII on his own elevation to the papacy in 1523 disclosed the existence of two bastard boys of putative Medicean parentage whom he installed at Florence as its future rulers under the guardianship of a Roman cardinal until they should reach maturity.

Far and away the most important of the supplementary political writings we are considering are the *Discourses on the First Ten Books of Livy*. They were begun in a leisurely way some years before a sudden impulse led to the composition of *The Prince,* and their amplification continued not improbably to the end of the author's days. At his death they had expanded into his work of greatest extent, and so steadily has their reputation increased in recent years that in some quarters they have come to be regarded as a more valuable contribution to political philosophy than the shorter work which still everywhere recalls his name.

Titus Livius devoted a long and studious life to the writing of his *History of Rome.* It became a classic of the Augustan Age, a kind of prose counterpart to Virgil's famous poetical epic. Of the one hundred and forty-two books of which it was composed at its completion only thirty-five have sur-

vived, among which the first ten, covering the earlier centuries of the city's history, constitute the most important
single fragment. Livy was an old-fashioned republican who
reluctantly, under the wooing of Augustus, made his peace
with the victorious principate. In his view the original primitive shepherd settlement on the Tiber owed its gradual consolidation as well as its astonishing upward surge to world
eminence to the moral stamina of its inhabitants and to an
unwavering devotion to the protective circle of its gods. Unfailing attachment to these two fundamental features issued
in a republican form of government, which continued to
prevail until the rise of selfish and ambitious politicians
brought about the long civil war of the first century B.C. in
which the republic perished.

The new learning or humanist age in which he was born
caused Machiavelli to saturate himself with classical literature, and his inborn passion for politics led him more particularly to the study of history and in a peculiarly intensive
manner to Roman history and its leading classical expositor,
Titus Livius. In his comments or *Discourses,* as he called
them, in which his regard for Livy culminated, he speaks
of the deep respect for the recovered learning of antiquity
prevailing in his lifetime and notes how the current legal
systems as well as the current medical practices are manifest
derivations from the classical originals. Why then had the
political experiences of antiquity failed to leave their mark
on contemporary political institutions, although their record
was once again, after the long medieval eclipse in general
circulation, exposed to everyone's view in the classical literature? Ascribing the anomaly to mental indolence, he an-
nounces his intention to put an end to a disgraceful situa-

tion by a running commentary on the first ten books of Livy which have survived in their entirety and, in order to facilitate a firmer grasp of the underlying principles, to embrace within his purview modern as well as ancient political developments.

It is a happy circumstance that throughout the *Discourses* we encounter a Machiavelli who, speaking solely for himself, sets forth none but his own direct and unqualified convictions. Consequently it does not take long to discover that he as passionately approved of the Roman republic as he abominated the later Empire; that he inclined to a popular form of government because it alone was dedicated to the common good; that the final and conclusive reason for his preferring the republic was that it rested on moral and religious principles constituting the solid foundation of the Roman and every other prosperous society. We are also before long made aware that the author's reflections, ranging beyond the early centuries treated in Livy's first ten books, ended by embracing the total course of Roman history. This brought about a discrepancy between title and subject matter which can be plausibly explained. While starting his study with the early books of Livy, he unconsciously extended his range without troubling to change his title, and his heirs, on undertaking after his death to publish a work never brought to a formal termination, clung to the label they found appended to the original manuscript.

More abundantly than in any other of his works the *Discourses* supply the ground for defining Machiavelli primarily as a political philosopher. What he offers in them are political deductions from the richly contentious development of the city on the Tiber intended to serve as guides to the understanding, first, of Roman history and, by implication, of all human societies whatever. For, according to Machiavelli and, by the way, according to Thucydides before him, man is everywhere and at all times essentially the same creature. While it will be impossible to do justice to the immense reflective wealth of the *Discourses,* a liberal sampling is indispensable and may as well begin with recording the author's view of the invaluable consequence of the unbroken struggle for control between the patricians, intrenched in the Senate as in a walled fortress, and the steadily growing mass of the abused common people, the plebeians. At times the angry conflict went to such lengths that the plebeians abandoned the city in order to wring from their stubborn masters a concession on which they had set their hearts. Only by slow stages did the plebeians enforce their various claims, following their first major triumph of achieving the appointment of two officials, called "Tribunes," charged to act as their defenders whenever a clash with the patricians took place. Instead of deploring these unceasing conflicts, Machiavelli's insight enabled him to grasp that continued healthy conflict led to healthy compromise and that it was compromise that accounted for Roman political liberty and for the relatively long stretch of time that liberty endured.

Equally enlightened is Machiavelli's indorsement of the official called "dictator." Granted that his appointment was a step in the direction of monarchy, his period of power was always strictly circumscribed, and he was pledged to retire as soon as the emergency to which he owed his elevation had passed. Nevertheless, the dictator was a threat hanging over the republic which remained innocuous only for so long a period as Roman society retained its original integrity. When the city fell into a settled corruption, this office became the tool enabling a succession of ambitious politicians to make the republic unworkable until it had been transformed into a monarchy.

Since corruption is for Machiavelli the turning point in the history of Rome, it would be interesting to get his view as to how corruption originated. Like the ancients before him, he made little of the influence on politics of economic factors, although he does name riches as a growing source of evil at Rome, especially so when coupled with the love of enduring power nursed by party leaders. These two related agencies, riches and ambition, led to the weakening of the moral fiber of the citizen body, both of patricians and plebeians, and terminated in the fateful civil war that put an end to the republic. This to him lamentable development does not shake his settled, dogmatic position that founders of a republic invite praise, founders of a tyranny, execration. It is this attitude which explains why, although fully aware that the republic was already doomed before Caesar's arrival on the scene, he felt impelled to indulge his passionate republicanism by cursing Caesar as the republic's murderer and extolling Brutus as its hapless last and noble champion. Once more it is seen, as stated at the outset, that he was not an instinctive historian obliged by an inborn urge to shape an event according to the available evidence. His native bent was rather to squeeze the innumerable small occurrences making up the historical record, and meaningless in themselves, into generalizations calculated to throw light on the march of politics and to supply the responsible officials of later societies with useful directives in their labors.

In addition to statements like the foregoing group dealing exclusively with Roman growth and decline the *Discourses* carry an immense body of observations concerned with problems of government in general. A selection of them, proportioned to the dimensions of this essay, will serve to indicate their range and philosophical flavor. In chapter xlix (Book I) the difficulty in devising laws for the preservation of liberty is noted, for the illuminating reason that the loss of liberty is due to the corruption of manners and the corruption of manners is an area not particularly accessible to legislation. Chapter lv of the same book generalizes that republics cannot be established save in communities where a substantial social equality reigns; and chapter lviii makes the bold republican assertion that, in spite of the inconstancy of the multitude, the people in general are more prudent and stable and therefore more likely than an absolute ruler to display a sound judgment.

Not to spin out the author's abundant reflections to wearisomeness, let us content ourselves with pointing out that in the next division, Book II, chapter iii, we encounter the striking conclusion that Rome owed its greatness to its liberal policy of freely admitting strangers to citizenship; and this Roman policy is contrasted with the contrary policy of Sparta and Athens with its plainly debilitating consequences. Deeply concerned at all times with the problems of war, Machiavelli insisted (chap. xxiv)—and this remains a subject of debate even in our own day—that fortresses are often more injurious to a country than useful. Continuing his observations on war, he praises (chap. xxxiii) the Roman practice of leaving the commanders of armies already in the field entirely uncontrolled in their operations.

In his last book (Book III) he harks back to some of the moral issues that never ceased to engage his thinking. The desirability of poverty as opposed to riches in the citizen body is extolled (chap. xxv) by the famous example of Cincinnatus, who at the time of his appointment to the dictatorship was found by the emissaries of the Senate plowing his few acres with his own hands. In chapter xlii the author returns to an argument of *The Prince* which had aroused his contemporaries to red-hot fury by declaring that there was no disgrace in disregarding promises that were exacted by superior force. Chapter xlvii, almost the last item of these always noteworthy and often profitable political reflections, does honor to the loftiness of Machiavelli's patriotism, for it avows that love of country should make a good citizen forget whatever private wrongs he may have suffered at his country's hands.

It is clear that a man who devoted so much of his life to philosophical reflection must have had an artistic bent informing his speech and giving shape to his thought. However, Machiavelli was too closely concerned with the more material aspects of life represented by politics for his artistry to play a masterful role in his career or to do much more than to keep alive his interest in classical literature, an interest that so pervaded the intellectual circles of his age that it came to him as naturally as breathing. It is therefore no occasion for surprise to observe that he tried his hand at many varieties of verse, prompted by no higher purpose than to indulge a transient impulse. By such occasional excursions into literature he cannot be said to have done more than establish himself among his countrymen as a man of taste and cultivation.

But there was one literary genre for which he was so manifestly equipped by nature that, had he freely and steadily given himself to its practice, he might have reached a superior and even the supreme rank. This inborn talent pointed to the comedy of manners, which he was hindered from pursuing freely by the current blind worship of classical models. Under the ruling humanist obsession the accepted and unapproached masters in the comedy field were Plautus and Terence; and so submissively did Machiavelli himself acknowledge their supremacy that only in a single instance did he venture to step out from under their shadow. This occurred when he wrote the piece called *Mandragola*. Its quality is so definitely Italian and even narrowly Florentine that it not only promptly took its place at the head of the native productions in this field but has held it to the present day. In the seventeenth century the Frenchman Molière achieved the happiest expression ever attained in this particular comedy form. It is not making an excessive claim for Machiavelli to hail him as an Italian precursor of the famous Frenchman.

The theme of *Mandragola* descends in direct line from the tales of Boccaccio and is consequently so stripped of the generally accepted social conventions as to carry, at least for non-Latin ears, a touch of the illicit and even obscene. With this obstacle—if it is an obstacle—overcome by the reader, the path is cleared for the play of character which is the core of the piece and which is so vivaciously sustained as to yield a harvest of pure amusement. The plot turns about an aging Florentine and his young wife who, as their supreme wish, hope to have the child thus far denied them and who become the victims of a company of waggish scoundrels, propounders of an outrageous plan to bring the couple's dearest hope to fulfilment. We may assume that it is an expression of the author's low opinion of the clergy that the only definitely evil member of the conspiracy is a priest. However, it reveals Machiavelli's artistry that the priest is shown as an actual human being without any attempt to distort him in order to drive home a moral lesson. Like all the other characters of the play he is presented, so to speak, in the state of nature. The spectator (or reader) is left entirely free to draw his own moral conclusions, if any, from the intrigue he is witnessing. The author's sole concern has been to provide, along with legitimate amusement, artistic enlightenment on literature's inexhaustible theme of human nature by the exhibition of actual men and women involved in a closely shared experience.

While it was indispensable to disclose the mental range of Machiavelli by taking account of him as a humanist and comic artist, it would be a mistake to close a review of his activities on this note. His main concern throughout life was politics, and his main purpose as a writer was to bring some sort of order into the unmanageable torrent of uninterrupted political events by assembling them under reflections and generalizations by which their total movement acquired at least a measure of intelligibility and could without presumption be offered to the masters and lords of politics in the expectation that they might profit from them by establishing a more effective control of public affairs. The vast preponderance of Machiavelli's writing revolves around this single interest, and its two shining works are *The Prince* and the *Discourses on the First Ten Books of Livy*. Their perusal reveals that, while he labored on them in the detached spirit of the scientific investigator, he was kept faithful to his purpose by the passionate heartbeat of his Florentine and Italian patriotism. Search as one will, no better summary of his total effort can be found than by the designation of Machiavelli as a political philosopher in the title of this essay; but let it never be forgotten that in the long succession of the world's political philosophers he carries the distinguishing mark of a warm-hearted lover of his country—a country which had sunk in his time to the intolerable role of a plaything and victim of the great powers of Europe.

BIBLIOGRAPHICAL NOTE

Of the many complete editions of Machiavelli's works, the one here used is the following: *Niccolò Machiavelli Opere a cura di Antonio Panella* (2 vols.; Rizzoli, Milano-Roma). Other works used were: Allan H. Gilbert, *The Prince and Other Works* (Chicago: Packard & Co., 1941); *The Prince and the Discourses,* with an Introduction by Max Lerner (New York: Modern Library, 1950); Arthur L. Burd, *Il Principe di N. Machiavelli* (Oxford, 1891); Jeffrey Pulver, *Machiavelli: The Man, His Work, and His Times* (London, 1937); Pasquale Villari, *The Life and Times of N. Machiavelli,* translated by Linda Villari (London, 1878).

VOLTAIRE

The Voice of Rationalism

In the course of a long life of tireless activity Voltaire became the dynamic center of French and, finally, of European eighteenth-century thought. It is not an exaggeration to say that, more perhaps than anyone before or since, he epitomized his age. Many phases of development, some of which will be indicated in these pages, contributed to the winning of this distinction. Voltaire's youth and young manhood lay under the sunset glow of the great age of Louis XIV. Thus his first passionate purpose was to employ the literary talent wherewith he was endowed by nature to follow in the footsteps of the *grands écrivains* of the brilliant immediate past and, more particularly, of the tragic poets Corneille and Racine. As early as 1718, when he was still only twenty-four years old, he produced the tragedy *Œdipe* and found himself publicly acclaimed as their indubitable successor.

Even before his play had won him an early literary fame, he had grown critical of the social environment in which he was imbedded and amused himself with witty sallies against its provocative absurdities, in the frivolous spirit fashionable among the circle of libertine young nobles with whom he habitually associated. While these highborn gentlemen welcomed the commoner to their company because of their delight in his sparkling conversation, they did not fail, or at least some coarser spirits among them did not fail, to keep him aware of the social chasm that yawned between them and him. Out of this repressed but ever present social tension there developed a bitter feud between the born bourgeois and an arrogant member of the great Rohan family. Its upshot was Voltaire's arrest and detention in the Bastille under an arbitrary royal order called *lettre de cachet,* which the nobleman's influence was able to invoke against his adversary. The victim won his release after a short imprisonment on his promise to go into voluntary exile.

Of the many capricious turns in his career this ranks as the master turn, for it carried him to England and led to his transformation from a young, high-spirited wit discharging an occasional malicious dart against the staring evils of the French socio-political order into its passionate opponent, dedicated to an unrelenting advocacy of a systematic program of reform. The change came about because, on setting foot in the island kingdom, his alert intelligence at once discerned the prevalence of a measure of rationality unknown as yet on the Continent and of thence derived institutional changes which had delivered England from some of the worst abuses handed down from the past. What particularly struck the visitor was the replacement of the absolute monarchy, exercising an arbitrary power symbolized by the *lettre de cachet,* with a constitutional system secured and guaranteed by an elected parliament. From this there followed a reign of law with habeas corpus protecting the individual against arbitrary arrest; an aristocracy completely subjected to the laws of the state; and a flourishing trade conducted by a merchant class enjoying the respect of a government which frankly accepted the pursuit of material prosperity as a leading public concern. And what probably especially invited the exile's admiration was the relatively high measure of religious toleration enjoyed by Englishmen, in spite of the existence of a privileged national church.

Voltaire's residence in England lasted about two and a half years, from 1726 to 1729, when he returned to France. Converted from an impulsive and occasional to a reasoning and unwavering critic of inherited abuses, he undertook to set forth the advances scored by English society in a work called *Lettres philosophiques* or *Sur les anglais,* published in 1734. The English improvements therein enumerated were by an unspoken but transparent implication advocated for France. Never afterward abandoned, his championship of reform thenceforth definitely overshadowed his earlier poetic ambition. Let this not be understood, however, to signify that he lost his interest in dramatic production; for it is an outstanding fact that he continued to write plays, chiefly tragedies, to the end of his days. A never to be overlooked characteristic of this indefatigable worker was that on taking up a new form of thought or expression he would add it to the interests already in hand. Consequently he cultivated an ever increasing variety of social and literary fields as long as he lived.

The next turn in Voltaire's fortunes was less a novelty than an intellectual consolidation of his newly acquired interest in reform. In the year of the publication of his *Lettres philosophiques,* he followed a beloved woman, Madame du Châtelet, to her estate of Cirey in eastern France and made Cirey his headquarters until her death fifteen years later. The lady, gushingly apostrophized by him as *la divine Émilie,* was one of the most astonishing women of her or any time, for she was fervidly given to the cause of rational self-education, generally supposed to be reserved to men, by an intense application to mathematics, science, and philosophy. Before long her relation to Voltaire assumed the character less of a love affair than of an intellectual companionship dedicated to the pursuit of the recent development of the natural sciences as exemplified by Isaac Newton and of philosophy as propounded by John Locke. There can be no doubt that, under the inspired guidance of his hostess, Voltaire achieved a mastery of advanced modern thought which enabled him to build his reform activity on a solid objective foundation.

Even before the inauguration of the Cirey episode Voltaire had become interested in history, as is proved by his publishing in 1731 his first venture in this field, the life of Charles XII, king of Sweden. The book was composed largely from anecdotal material supplied by diplomats who had had occasion to deal professionally with the famous monarch. Voltaire was at the time still ruled by his original literary passion and was attracted to Charles XII as a conspicuous example of the tragic hero, who, after rising to the height of

glory, landed in the depths of defeat. The extraordinary
vivacity with which the story was presented won it an in-
stantaneous success and has secured it a body of readers
down to our day. This is a tribute to the incomparable light-
ness and grace of the author's style. However, these formal
merits are unable to conceal the weakness of the work as
history. Voltaire untiringly sounds his hero's courage, daring, and stubborn persistence in a once adopted course of
action, that is, in an impressive sum of military virtues
which he conspicuously failed to match with equivalent
civilian wisdom. While Voltaire did not cast a veil over this
deficiency, he failed to elaborate it as the main explanation
of his hero's ultimate catastrophe. Furthermore, by entirely
overlooking Charles's specific Swedish background, he had
him emerge from a social vacuum. These defects suffice to
prove that the author was at the time of composition a historical novice who had yet to achieve a mature view of politics and society.

Voltaire's flashing brilliance has sometimes led to his being
charged with superficiality. True, he was often superficial,
owing to his quick and impulsive nature. However, en-
tranced with history after his first wayward taste of it, he
thenceforth gave himself so wholeheartedly to serious historical study that he ended by becoming the foremost historian of his time and rose besides to the distinction of winning a place among the select company of historical inno-
vators. Since it is not the purpose of this essay to treat the
total work of Voltaire but only his historical achievement,
the phases of his development thus far traced could not im-
properly be terminated at this point. But having embarked
on a swift indication of the steady enlargement of his outlook

and activity, it is hardly permissible to overlook his last phase wherein he figured as the sage of Ferney.

Ferney was an estate in eastern France, on the border of the free state of Geneva, which Voltaire acquired when he had already reached the advanced age of sixty-five. Its closeness to Geneva was a leading factor in its purchase, since it enabled him to slip across the French border into safety whenever he found himself threatened, as he never ceased to be, by the French police. Ferney became the acknowledged literary capital of Europe for the next nineteen years, until its master's death in 1778. It was visited by an almost uninterrupted stream of people who, either converted to or well disposed toward Voltaire's rationalism, looked on him as though rationalism had become a religion and he its hallowed saint. Relatively secure from governmental interference because of his fame, Voltaire intensified his war on the persistent, hoary abuses in law, economics, and society and boldly denounced in pamphlets and books of a tingling vitality the conspicuous universal, but also the numerous national, instances of scandalous breaches of reason and the shocking iniquities that invariably attended them.

While it is hoped that this introductory review will serve as a useful backdrop to Voltaire's far-ranging mind, let it again be said that this study is not concerned with the total magnitude of the man but only with his role as a historian. Undeniably, however, the setting forth of even that limited role will necessitate close attention to certain facts and ventures of a personal nature which bore directly on the shaping of his character and indirectly on his development as a writer of histories.

The earliest of these formative facts touches his birth and family. He was born on November 21, 1694, in the heart of Paris. Although an infant so feeble that his life was despaired of and although more or less ailing as long as he lived, there must have been a tough core to him, for he survived to the advanced age of eighty-four years. His family name was Arouet, which on becoming a writer he dropped for that of Voltaire. Promptly acquiring a reputation under this pen name, he adopted the name also for general use; finally, his real name was practically forgotten. How he arrived at the choice of Voltaire is in dispute among scholars, but the most commonly held view is that it is an anagram of Arouet, with the letters *l* and *j* (standing for *le jeune,* the younger) added to distinguish him from his father. In any case it is under his invented and not under his family name that the great Frenchman figures in history.

Arouet the elder was a notary of standing who served as legal adviser to families of means, many of whom belonged to the nobility. Identified thus as a member of the prosperous upper bourgeoisie, the son was enrolled in the famous Jesuit college Louis-le-Grand, which, since it was favored by the aristocracy, enabled him to establish an early intimacy with many of its sons. His practical father planned to have him follow in his footsteps, but the son objected so vigorously that a crisis resulted which was resolved only after a violent conflict ending with the son having his way. The immediate significance of this victory was that, instead of associating with lawyers and tradesmen, he joined forces with a group of young noblemen who, lifted by their hereditary privileges above the common herd, regarded themselves as the salt of the earth. They encouraged Voltaire's ambition to emulate

Racine and helped to make his first tragedy, *Œdipe,* a popular success. As we have already seen, they also stimulated him to vie with them in lighthearted, frivolous taunting of a backward government and church. Finally, as we have further noted, his love feast with his social superiors terminated in a disastrous conflict with one of them and in his enforced departure for England.

From Voltaire's English exile dates his rise to leadership in the cause of rational reform, to which, although it is not our main concern, occasional reference will be unavoidable, since it is so firmly woven into the texture of his life. It was also in England that he picked up some of the current gossip about the astonishing Charles XII of Sweden, so that England may claim to have had a part in starting him off as a historian.

Although no better than apprentice work, the biography of Charles II so infatuated Voltaire with history that he took to greedily devouring all available works dealing with the past of mankind. Convinced by his penetrating intelligence of their prevailingly unreliable and trivial character, he acquired the habit of going, as far as possible, behind the published version of an event to its documentary source. It did not take him long to choose as his first solid undertaking in the new field of interest the culminating period of his own country, the glamor of which still lingered in the sky, the reign of Louis XIV. And since Louis dominated not only France but Europe as well, the alert scholar gave his attention from the first less to a reign than to a period or age. It is established that he began his labors on Louis XIV in 1732, immediately after Charles XII was off his hands, and that he patiently assembled and diligently screened his materials as

100

the obligatory scholarly service preliminary to conscientious composition. The finished book, under the title *Le Siècle de Louis XIV,* made its appearance only after twenty years of dedicated labor. It has been calculated that he drew for it on two hundred volumes of printed memoirs in addition to some still in manuscript, including the most famous of them all, the memoirs of the Duke of Saint-Simon. Fully aware of the slips of memory and the distorting personal bias inseparable from this form of literature, he drew on memoirs only after subjecting them to the most searching criticism. On receiving, through the usual channel of private influence at court, the appointment of official historiographer of France, he was able to extend his researches by using the free access to the state archives that his office afforded him.

The Age of Louis XIV on publication promptly leaped to a fame which it has held practically unimpaired to this day. It is therefore not surprising that both composition and content have drawn the professional attention of a long chain of scholars. Without exception they have given praise to the author's zeal, industry, and critical acumen. At the same time they have been in agreement over the far more important achievement that with this book Voltaire had created a new historical form. According to these scholars, not only did he abandon the chronicle type of history inherited from the Middle Ages and still in general use throughout Europe, but he also, although admiring the ancients, emphatically rejected their narrow view that history's leading or even its sole concern was with politics. To prove their point these scholars have referred to the statement in Voltaire's Preface that history's true objective was the tastes and manners of the peoples of the earth and the orderly advance attributable to their organized societies. To emphasize their argument they have cited his further statement that in his work his attention was riveted "not on the actions of a single man but on the spirit of man in the most enlightened age which has ever been." Since "enlightenment" meant to him, first of all, the rule of rationality or at least some active measure of it and, after that, the enrichment of life through literature and the arts, he had all the justification he needed for ascribing to the age of Louis XIV its exalted status. In short, his critics have incontestably established that Voltaire widened the scope of history from politics to civilization and that by so doing he had harked back, after a neglect of twenty centuries, to the "Father of History," to Herodotus, who in a far more naïve and rambling manner, it is true, pursued an identical purpose.

If we now turn to the *Siècle* itself, we shall discover that it carries influences and features of the past which make it considerably less that novelty, a history of civilization, than most commentators, overwhelmed by Voltaire's indubitable increase of scope, have confidently asserted. Nor does Voltaire on undertaking the objective presentation of the facts regularly present an image of them which is beyond cavil. But why, one asks, should his occasional lapse from his announced approach be taken too seriously when every historian has fallen short of perfection both in carrying out his own avowed purpose and in realizing the indisputably final shape of the events he has been engaged in depicting. This writer does not hesitate to affirm that the book's first two chapters, which hurriedly review the condition of France and Europe before the advent of Louis XIV, and the four subsequent chapters as well, which deal more in the ancient chronicle fashion than with Voltaire's subsequently displayed clarity with the French civil war called the Fronde, are unworthy of his reputation. Not until chapter vii, where he has King Louis personally assume the government and at once reveal his fateful arrogance by obliging every rival European monarch to yield him precedence, does Voltaire fairly get his teeth into his matter. He closes the seventh chapter ominously with the sentence that serves as the leitmotif of the whole subsequent political story: "Louis was young, rich, well served, blindly obeyed, and full of impatience to win distinction, to become a conqueror."

Under no circumstances to be overlooked is the fact that, with this earliest chapter dealing with the central figure of his book, Voltaire, like the ancients before him, launches on straight political history, which by reason of his never failing vivacity he makes a wholly engaging tale. Once thus engaged, he cannot again let go, with the result that it is the political history of Louis XIV and his time that by actual count of pages makes up the bulk of his book. Nor would any sensible person wish it to be otherwise, since, even when history is expanded to the concept of civilization, political history is bound to remain an important, and perhaps even the most important, single element in its complicated structure. The point needing to be made and stressed is that, when Voltaire raised his sights to take in the whole of civilization, he was not prompted to reject the long-standing traditional view regarding the significant role of politics in history.

If Voltaire's treatment of political history has won him an enduring acclaim, the reason usually given is the ease, grace, and vigor of his style. He aimed, above all, at readability, an aim present-day so-called "scientific" historians hardly ever any longer entertain. In his view the unpardonable sin for anyone who took pen in hand was to be a bore. But of at least equal importance with his lively style is the mind behind the style, the essentially rational mind which he had studiously cultivated from his youth onward. It lifted him to an outlook over Europe as from a mountaintop and enabled him to maintain, save for very rare lapses, a balanced judgment between France, the aggressor power, and the fluttered dovecot of its European neighbors. Voltaire was at heart a warm French patriot—let there be no mistake on that score. Consequently he took an unconcealed pride in the worldwide eminence his country had won by reason of its literature, its arts and crafts, its manners and fashions, and particularly its language, which had been shaped by its writers into a medium of expression of unrivaled precision and flexibility.

His exultation over this dominance—a dominance, let it be noted, strictly of the spirit—not infrequently broke through even in the political section of his book. Agreed, it does not belong there any more than does the on occasion insufficiently veiled favor with which he viewed Louis's early military triumphs. He was, after all, a human being with every human being's emotional shortcomings. His established rational outlook should have moved him to love peace and abhor war, and, generally speaking, his attitude strictly conformed to these terms; but, launched at the start of Louis's aggression on the strikingly successful campaigns conducted by such brilliant generals as Condé and Turenne, he was in his role of narrator swept off his feet and—almost in his own despite, one is tempted to say—represented war as the glorious enterprise it was universally held to be. But when after three decades of unhalted French aggression a solidly united Europe at last, in the War of the Spanish Succession, turned against the perpetual disturber of its peace and by slow, relentless pressure completely broke the French power, Voltaire recovered his normal judgment and denounced war in the bitterest terms. The War of the Spanish Succession is the climax of the political portion of Voltaire's history and shows him at his best in his analysis of men and events and in the sheer lucidity and animation of his storytelling.

It also shows his manner of portraiture. Taking his cue in this respect from the ancients, he regarded the presentation of the leading personages of the drama he was engaged in unfolding as an obligatory feature of his work. For so subtle a spirit his method was disappointingly bare and factual, since it consisted, in the main, in nothing more than listing the leading incidents of his subject's life. It was a procedure sharply at variance with the psychological penetration demanded by the taste of the present day; however, it cannot be denied that his portraits show a clean profile and come vividly to life. While the statement applies particularly to the Frenchmen of the story, to King Louis with his attendant staff of officers and administrators, it holds as well for the opponents of France, such as the Duke of Marlborough, Prince Eugene of Austria, and the republican John de Witt of Holland, whom Voltaire, with conspicuous fairmindedness, delighted to endow with the full complement of their merits.

Not till after Voltaire had completed the political story of Louis XIV did he undertake to survey the many other areas of French life and society, thus extending the range of history as then practiced and achieving the distinction of becoming the first modern historian of civilization. The political history of the book covers the Peace of Utrecht, which terminated the War of the Spanish Succession, and closes with the death, three years later, in 1715, of the chastened and greatly diminished Roi Soleil. The following four chapters, while labeled "Anecdotes," are something far more important than that word conveys, since they present a picture of French society in Louis's day. Regrettably they do not concern themselves with the lower orders, with the bourgeoisie and the peasants. Not for a moment is it to be supposed that Voltaire had no interest in these fellow countrymen who constituted the overwhelming majority of the population and of whom he was one. The whole course of his life is crowded with convincing evidence to the contrary. But the writings from which he drew the material for these particular chapters were memoirs; and memoirs, practically without exception, were written by members of the French ruling class and dealt with the interests, the rivalries, the conflicts, the amusements, and the scandals that filled their days. Consequently what we get is very one-sided—the life of the court and the aristocracy. However, it costs no effort to bow to this limitation, since never before or since were court and aristocracy so brilliant a phenomenon and so calculated to excite a justifiable curiosity.

A further feature of these anecdotal chapters, bound to strike even casual readers and sure to irritate systematic ones, is that, strung together from excerpts clipped from memoirs, they are conspicuously lacking in orderly development. While they indeed treat, as stated, of court and aristocracy, a close scrutiny will disclose that what Voltaire had chiefly in mind in shaping them was to set forth the private life of

Louis XIV as the fitting counterpart to his public life developed in the preceding political section. We therefore get a frequently broken but essentially coherent tale, beginning with the bodily grace and spiritual glamor of the young monarch and continuing with the successive charmers who served as his officially acknowledged mistresses at the side of the Spanish-born queen to whom Louis never failed to pay the at least outward respect due to her station. At the same time the delighted narrator unfolds the never-before-heard-of magnitude and luxury of the spectacles and masques which the young sovereign staged to indulge the court's love of pleasure and, perhaps even more, his own unrestrained self-dramatization. Owing to what we may call the garrulous form of composition which Voltaire adopted for these anecdotal chapters, he felt free, whenever the spirit prompted, to interpolate material foreign to his main matter but deserving attention for its own sake. Among such intrusions figures the famous mystery story of the "Man with the Iron Mask," which Voltaire, conscientious scholar that he was, sets forth with such scrupulous regard for the ascertainable facts that it may be recommended as a model of reporting to all delvers into tantalizing historical mysteries.

However, the abiding object of attention of the four chapters under discussion is the person of Louis XIV, for whom Voltaire, while frankly revealing his errors and weaknesses, exhibits a sincere respect. He makes it clear that never, in his view, had the role of king been enacted so superbly and never had the stately play acting been matched with a more unshaken devotion to the tireless labor demanded by an office which, by Louis's own conviction, was both an honor and a burden bestowed on him from on high. It is with the same deep respect that Voltaire deals with Madame de Maintenon, who in Louis's middle years effected the major miracle of cleansing him of his loose sexual habits and who then put the seal on the reform she had wrought by being secretly joined to him in matrimony some five years after his Spanish-born queen's death.

Voltaire's admiration for Louis XIV reached a climax when, following his crushing defeat in the War of the Spanish Succession, the king developed a dignity of a far higher moral order than that of the inflated pomp employed in his earlier years to express his conception of grandeur. It is not easy to forget the scene our author presents of Louis on his deathbed, when, surrounded by his court, he addressed the puny prince, his five-year-old great-grandson destined to succeed him, in these solemn terms: "Try to preserve peace with your neighbors. I have loved war too much. Do not imitate me in that nor in the excessive expenditures in which I indulged." In this dying confession of error there is a humility that makes it possible for later ages to join Voltaire in his feeling of respect for a king with absolute power—for a type of ruler for whom the living generation has neither understanding nor sympathy.

The remaining chapters of the book take up what we may call "domestic" France and describe, in terms which a later, better-informed scholarship has revised in numerous details, the many distinct sections of national life. Voltaire, turning first to government, describes the administrative improvements effected under Louis XIV together with the financial, commercial, and industrial reforms carried through by the great Colbert, the founder, or at least a leading exponent, of the contemporary economic philosophy known as "mercantilism." With respect to mercantilism, which preaches the promotion of industry, commerce, and agriculture by government favors and subsidies, a comment of Voltaire deserves to be quoted as illustrative of his characteristic common sense: "It is not gold or silver that ensures the comforts of life but personal initiative." Associated with Colbert among Louis's leading cabinet members was Louvois, to whom was due the conversion of the traditional small mercenary force maintained by the kings of France to a steadily swelling standing army divided into numerous increasingly specialized services. It was from a humane angle an unhappy innovation, since it obliged the neighboring countries to imitate it in order not to be hopelessly outmatched in the field. From Louvois's creation to our own time the standing army has been an inescapable feature of the organization of every European state.

Voltaire next took up science and philosophy, passing thence to the particularly congenial subjects of literature, music, and the fine arts. Indicative of a certain narrowness imposed on him by his rational outlook is his low regard for the literature inspired by religion in the ages preceding his own. The romantically inspired century that followed the rationalist period has effectively modified this derogatory estimate.

With a mind alerted from boyhood against the intolerant orthodoxy of the Catholic church, he could not fail to give it throughout his life a searching attention and to take careful note of the usually hidden but occasionally open struggle between the church and the state over the ultimate control of the nation. His religious survey carried him in due course to the heretical Huguenots and the attempt by Louis XIV to totally suppress them. As might be expected, Voltaire was free of any spontaneous affection for the stubbornly dogmatic followers of the rigorous Calvin. However, the revoltingly cruel measures adopted to blot them from the face of France aroused his burning indignation, since their foreseeable effect was to persuade the inhumanly persecuted sect, rather than yield, to abandon the country and carry their industrial skill and intellectual energy to the neighboring countries, whose inhabitants met them at the boundaries with open arms.

The book ends with a moral lesson. Voltaire had ranged with his historical reading all the way to the empire of China, and he had learned that religious peace had reigned there for centuries owing to a settled policy of toleration on the part of the government. He had learned how even Christian missionaries had been welcomed until the intolerance inherent in their doctrinal foundations had induced hitherto unknown civil commotions and had caused their eviction from the country. It was peculiarly appropriate that a history of France, inspired by a rationalist philosophy and unwaveringly critical of the reigning Christian intolerance, should be brought to a close with a historical example of a truly liberalized society drawn not from Europe but from distant Asia.

Le Siècle de Louis XIV made its official appearance in 1752, while Voltaire was residing at Berlin as the honored guest of King Frederick II of Prussia, known afterward as Frederick the Great. Owing to the absence of both national and international copyright, the work, like all the works of the most popular writers of the period, was promptly reproduced in a sizable number of piratical editions. Frederick, yielding, while still crown prince, to the unbounded admi-

ration he felt for the French writer, had opened a correspondence with the object of his adoration. After becoming
king in 1740 he repeatedly pressed Voltaire to make his
home with him; but not until 1749, when Voltaire, on the
death of Madame du Châtelet, lost his only secure footing
in France, did he give ear to the invitation. He arrived in
Berlin in July, 1750, and departed in a cloud of scandal some
two and a half years later. The episode constitutes one of
the most exciting adventures of Voltaire's adventurous life
but must, except for a summary statement, be passed over
here as having no bearing on our theme of Voltaire the
historian.

After the break occurred it was clear to every reflective
spirit that the love feast with which the union of the two
apparently congenial souls was inaugurated could not last.
While Frederick was a crowned king by right of birth, Voltaire was an uncrowned king of letters by right of genius,
and the two kingships of a fundamentally different order
were bound to develop a friction inevitably terminating in
a conflagration. The Berlin story has been treated at length
in all the histories dealing with one or the other of the two
protagonists, each of whom was the towering figure of the
period in the field of activity to which he had been called by
either fate or natural endowment. For this writer the episode
as recounted by Carlyle in his *History of Frederick the Great*
surpasses all other versions because of Carlyle's incomparable gift for drama. His tale of the gathering storm runs the
gamut all the way from tragedy or near-tragedy to hilarious
buffoonery injected into the situation by Voltaire's lam-
poons—the wittiest this master of wit ever composed. In
this anonymously circulated satire he mercilessly took apart

111

a rival Frenchman alike high in Prussian office and in Frederick's esteem. Carlyle's vivacious presentation is so notably fair to the two principals of the clash that each emerges with his character temporarily tarnished but essentially intact.

The most important effect on Voltaire of the Berlin fiasco was the resolution never again to accept the patronage of a royal master, no matter how alluring the proffered advantages might be. Determined henceforth to cherish his independence as the supreme good, he looked about after his escape from Prussia for a property whereof he would be the unchallenged master. He found it at last in Ferney where, as we have already learned, he spent his closing years, a busy landlord, engaged in a dozen projects for improving his land and buildings, and a generous host, receiving in an endless procession the homage of the enlightened representatives of every nation of Europe. While never ceasing to pursue the historical studies which had indisputably won the first place in his affections, he remained faithful to every form of expression to which he had ever applied his genius. The statement is eminently true of tragedy, in spite of the fact that the acclaim he gained with his pieces was so ephemeral that during the next, the nineteenth, century they had without exception vanished from the stage. It is pathetic evidence of his own consistent overrating of his theater work that on his last much-feted visit to Paris, in his eighty-fifth year, he had brought with him in his baggage his latest fabrication, *Irène*. If the issue be raised why his poetic dramas, sixteen in all, have been swept into oblivion, let the answer be suggested in the query: Has great poetry or, rather, has the greatest poetry which lives on effortlessly from generation to generation ever been written by a rationalist?

So inexhaustible was Voltaire's mental energy that he constantly experimented with new literary forms, the outstanding invention of his middle period being the *conte philosophique.* In this genre his most famous production was *Candide,* a work which has retained the favor of succeeding generations down to our day. While a tale of fantastically jumbled adventure, it is in its central purpose a satire on the blind optimism championed by a number of philosophically inspired contemporaries. The English poet Alexander Pope had made himself a mouthpiece of the current optimist patter when, in his *Essay on Man,* he had declared: "Whatever is, is right." And the philosopher Leibniz had raised himself to the position of banner-bearer of the cult when he drew from his conviction that creation was the work of a wholly beneficent deity the conclusion that the world wherein we live was necessarily "the best of all possible worlds." Although Voltaire was not a cynic, even though his free-ranging mind often invited that accusation, his common sense, which was one of his happiest endowments, was offended by a description of our existence in terms so little in accord with the observable facts, and he undertook to make sport of the Leibniz-Pope philosophy by elaborating some of the innumerable mishaps which are the inescapable attendants of our chance-directed earthly pilgrimage.

While still engaged in mastering the materials for *The Age of Louis XIV,* and long before the completion of the work, Voltaire had become aware that the period he was treating remained inexplicable save in the light of the period that preceded it—the Middle Ages. Consequently he extended his studies to this earlier age, the dark seedbed not only of French but of all European civilization. But why restrict his investigations to the small western extension of the Asiatic land mass, commonly called Europe, under the ancient delusion that its story was all there was to the essential story of mankind? Undeniably his predecessors in the field of history had contentedly limited themselves to Europe, with at best the southern and eastern coasts of the Mediterranean Sea thrown in for good measure. But the restless geographical discoverers, yielding to the fever excited in their blood by Diaz and Columbus and by the Christian missionaries following in the wake of the explorers' ships, had, beginning with the sixteenth century, penetrated far afield in Asia and, on their return to Europe, had published reports on such peoples as the Hindus and Malayans and especially on the most numerous and attractive of them all, the Chinese. Pursuant to an enlightening plunge into these surprising revelations, Voltaire once and for all dismissed the narrow, traditional opinion of the exclusive importance of the tiny continent of Europe and freely embraced Asia in his enlarged purview. This signified a radical change in perspective and viewpoint with the result that from his time on history, not at once, of course, but gradually, ceased to be Europe-centered and became world-centered.

Impelled by his expanded vision, Voltaire set about writing a history of the Middle Ages which he resolved to precede with at least a brief sketch of his startling discovery of the continent of Asia. He published the new work in 1756 under the title *Essai sur les Mœurs et l'Esprit des Nations et sur les Principaux Faits de l'Histoire depuis Charlemagne jusqu'à Louis XIII.* To the present writer the title was a most unhappy choice, in part, because of its inconvenient length and, in even larger part, because of its inaccuracy. For the work, instead of beginning, as announced, with Charlemagne, begins far more appropriately for a work on the Middle Ages with the origins of Christianity and the fall of the Roman Empire. It proceeds to offer as a kind of foreword to European medieval history an account, brief but remarkably illuminating for the time in which it was written, of the hitherto completely ignored Asiatic lands of China, India, Persia, and Arabia.

As the medieval raw material at Voltaire's disposal was of a slight and uncritical order, his version of the period became outmoded when with the nineteenth century an intense medieval scholarship made available in printed form a vast body of documents that permitted a precise formulation of the leading institutions and events of the period. However, in spite of its supersession, Voltaire's medieval history has the readability which characterizes all his prose writings, and it will always elicit an unfailing interest because of the rationalist bias with which it views the dominance of religion in an age celebrated as the age of faith. Writing from the point of view of this unconcealed bias, Voltaire's attention throughout the period is riveted on the usurpation of authority by the pope and the Catholic church —a usurpation made possible, according to Voltaire, by the crude, superstitious, and barbarous character of society. He is happy to note a revival of the arts, faint of course, beginning with the twelfth century, though the most absurd superstitions regrettably lived on unchecked. His solid principle of scholarship is revealed by a concluding declaration to the effect that the historian must avoid hearsay and rumor and let his version of an event be shaped exclusively by official documents and, where documents are not available, by the close checking of strictly contemporary statements against one another.

At the request of one of his many German admirers, the duchess of the small Thuringian state of Saxe-Gotha, he composed a history of Germany under the title *Annales de l'Empire*. It is such dull reading that it is impossible to believe that he did more than give directions to some secretary as to where to find the material and how to string it together into an old-fashioned chronicle. Such a procedure on his part would indicate a retreat from his habitual responsibility; but there are other instances of similar lapses, although of a far less flagrant character. The only other one of these lesser and dubious works requiring mention is the *Précis du Siècle de Louis XV*. Having worked backward from Louis XIV in his medieval history, he was almost inevitably prompted also to work forward from *Le Grand Monarque* to his very inferior successor, Louis XV. He was influenced also by the fact that his own life was to a large degree coextensive with this reign and that his characteristically intense absorption in all the happenings of his time enabled him to write its history without excessive and tiring documentary research. In consequence the *Précis* of Louis XV (note that he calls it not a history but a summary or outline) is more a journalist's than a historian's product. Its inferior quality was so quickly and generally recognized that it never occurred to anybody to pair it with its famous predecessor. However, the Voltairian touch is not wholly lacking, and it highlights a pedestrian tale with memorable passages. Among such may be recalled an account of the intolerable confusion caused by the continued coexistence in France of many different legal systems. A further continuing abuse was the practice of torture in criminal cases, coupled with judicial sentences so bloody and revolting that the quiet town squares usually chosen for carrying them out were metamorphosed into public slaughter houses. While the exposition of such monstrous medieval survivals definitely belongs to the realm of history, it also very properly falls under the rubric of rational reform, a cause to which Voltaire since his English exile had dedicated himself with priestly devotion and to which he remained faithful to his last breath.

In summarizing Voltaire's place as a historian, it would appear that his primary achievement was to re-establish history as a branch of literature and thus to raise it once more to the rank it had held among the ancients. The special significance of its recovered status was that, while it again became literature, it clearly defined itself as literature of a particular order. Its *raison d'être,* its acknowledged function, was to revive some segment of the human past by means of whatever direct evidence had chanced to survive. The critique of this evidence was called scholarship, the conscientious exercise of which might be counted on to supplant a fanciful with a more veracious picture of the past.

If scholarship was the first ingredient of Voltaire's history writing, there were two other ingredients of substantially equal value. The first of these was the lordship of language commonly called style, the second was a unifying point of view defined by him as "philosophy." There can be no doubt that the rich and ever lively flow of his speech was an outstanding reason for the enthusiasm with which his work was received by his contemporaries and which it still has the power to evoke. However, he always stoutly insisted that unless the historian, regardless of how masterfully he commanded the gift of speech, presented his story *en philosophe,* that is, unless he endowed the facts he recounted with an intelligible interpretation, his presentation would not rise above the level of a soulless chronicle.

It is on the ground of his third or subjective ingredient that Voltaire's history formula has usually been attacked, especially since the rise in the nineteenth century of the theory that history can and should be written with complete objectivity. This school of theorists has been overwhelmed by the certainty or seeming certainty of the natural sciences and has aspired to bring history to rest on general laws of an identical validity. Among American historians it was Henry Adams who made the stoutest effort to travel this path and thereby to transform history from an art into a science. The consensus among his colleagues is that Adams' labors ended in unmitigated failure. It throws a pathetic light on this failure that the New Englander's two enduring contributions to history, the one dealing with the administration of Jefferson and Madison, the other titled *Mont-Saint-Michel and Chartres,* are each solidified into a significant work of literature by a subjective cement. In the case of Voltaire the subjective cement, as this presentation has attempted to show, was rationalism, with all the consequent advantages and disadvantages of a particular and unchanging point of view. It seems clear and past challenge that what a ruling philosophy secures to a history is not truth absolute, which for the historian is forever unattainable, but a sustained intelligible sparkle of human meaning.

Voltaire's Catholic opponents never ceased to taunt him with being an atheist. But the charge will not stand, since he was an open and professed deist and, like deists in general, held the world to be the creation of a God who on completion of his handiwork set it in motion under a system of inalterable laws. For some reason which the deists shrewdly avoided to explain, God thereupon withdrew into himself or fell asleep or went ahunting and took no further interest in the affairs of his universe. All believing Christians, however, held fast to a diametrically opposed view that the vicissitudes that had in the past befallen mankind and would continue to befall it in the future had their origin in the unfathomed will of God. For Voltaire with his conception of a passive God the phenomenon of unceasing social change, which he regarded as the prime object of historical study, was simply not referable to his kind of deity. For him the only possible explanation of social movement was the will of human beings, whom he thus saluted as the shapers, for better or worse, of their own destiny. That it was not the traditionally Christian but Voltaire's purely rational outlook that finally won the day among professional writers of history is indicated by the fact that providence has so effectively been eliminated from present-day histories as no longer to be afforded even a cursory mention.

It would seem that Voltaire's view of the responsibility of mankind for its own success or failure should have made him an advocate of the political sytem called "democracy." This was far from being the case. In his picture of the march of history, and particularly of French history, the common people constituted the fighting force that the Catholic church had been able to mobilize against any movement that threatened its power. For Voltaire this situation remained unchanged as long as he lived and had not in any way been altered by the recent rise of the novel assumption of a continuous human progress. Undeniably the belief in progress which characterized the eighteenth century had been taken over by the European intelligentsia, and Voltaire himself was disposed to look on it with favor. However, having early arrived at the conviction that any improvement definable as progress that had ever been brought about was due to enlightened despotism, he could not, in the face of the facts as he read them, be persuaded to abandon his position. In his eyes Louis XIV was an enlightened despot, although unfortunately he fell sadly short of the possibilities inherent in his office. However, the century after Louis XIV bred an extraordinary crop of truly enlightened despots throughout Europe with many of whom, like Frederick II of Prussia, Catherine II of Russia, and a half-dozen minor German rulers, Voltaire had cultivated a flattering intimacy. In each of their dominions, whether large or small, these sovereigns had on their own authority and in spite of the opposition of the church and every other traditional institution effected an impressive record of reforms. The wellspring of their inspiration was a rational enlightenment, and rational enlightenment was a possession of the educated upper-class citizens and not of the masses.

Had Voltaire lived to the French Revolution, nothing would have surprised and shocked him so much as the attempted remodeling of society by the lower orders. The dynamic leaders of the Revolution were sharply aware of the point at which the road parted for themselves and him. While engaged in the early weeks after the opening of the

National Assembly with clearing the country of its antiquated institutions, these leaders praised Voltaire as the
hero who had shattered such institutions with a titan's ham-
mer before they ever had arrived on the scene. Then, on
taking up the task of shaping the fresh institutions destined
to replace the old, these same leaders pushed him violently
aside because the governmental system for which he had
consistently expressed a preference was monarchy. What
these forward-lookers aimed at was not monarchy but a republic, and the heaven-sent guide to that goal was a writer
who, though he had died some ten years before—in fact, in
the same year as Voltaire—was alive in every agitated soul
in France. His name was Jean Jacques Rousseau.

Rousseau, a Genevan by birth, was a younger member of
the same generation as Voltaire. He was a poor boy, highly
gifted, whom fate tossed about in the most disturbing
fashion and who never succeeded in winning a secure footing in society. While he had as a youth applauded Voltaire's
attack on traditional abuses, he never fully identified himself with him, since he rated the world of feeling in which he
lived as far more important than Voltaire's world of reason.
For him the trouble with society was not the debased institutions of a dying civilization but civilization itself. Back to
nature became his cry: *retournons à la nature.* And this cry
signified nothing less than that civilization itself was to be
abolished and society started on an entirely new development along purely natural lines. On projecting an ideal government in his *Social Contract,* he based it on a strict equal-
itarianism with all decisions made by the *volonté générale,*
that is, by the count of hands.

Rousseau thus became a link in the long succession of

121

projectors of utopias, all of whom without exception were anathema to Voltaire with his settled respect for a continuing culture resting, in last analysis, on reason and common sense. Consequently there gradually developed an open antagonism between these two most eminent proponents of reform, which on the outbreak of the French Revolution had its immediate reflection in the National Assembly. With the emotional fervor of the members of the assembly shared by the excited people whom they represented and mounting to ever new heights, it was inevitable that the modestly corrective proposals emanating from Voltaire should be completely engulfed by the glowing prospect of a never before realized human perfection held out by Rousseau.

The opposed reform purposes of Voltaire and Rousseau have continued to divide society to the present day. To the Voltairians among us the most precious possession of mankind is an inherited civilization which must imperatively and under all circumstances be preserved. However, since civilization is a continuous and infinitely complex process, a fresh development in one area is regularly matched by decay in another area, and this decay must needs be got rid of and, if necessary, rudely excised. To Rousseauists, however, fired with an overmastering emotional ideal, this corrective policy is a bungling and repulsive procedure. Far preferable, in their view, is it to treat the inherited civilization as waste and wreckage to be swept into total oblivion, thus clearing the ground for an entirely new social order. It takes no more than a pair of open eyes to see that Voltaire and Rousseau, each in his own way, are as alive and mutually exclusive today as they were in the French Revolution.

VOLTAIRE

BIBLIOGRAPHICAL NOTE

Voltaire's complete works (including dramas, prose tales, historical works, critical works, miscellaneous writings) have been repeatedly published. The edition employed here is that of Beuchot in seventy volumes. Convenient English translations of the *Life of Charles XII* and of *The Age of Louis XIV* will be found in the "Everyman's Library" edition. Excellent "lives" in English are by S. G. Tallentyre (1903) and R. Aldington (1925).

RANKE

Rise, Decline, and Persistence of a Reputation

The amazing spread and intensification of historical studies in the United States during the second half of the nineteenth century owed their main impetus to American scholars returning from Germany. It was in the leading German universities that American scholars had been refreshed and alerted by a new method of historical inquiry. At the head of the German movement was Professor Leopold Ranke of the University of Berlin. It was therefore in no way surprising that, when, in the year 1884, the ever widening stream of American interest led to the formation of the American Historical Association, its members should by a spontaneous act of homage have adopted the German master as their patron saint by welcoming him into their association as the first and only honorary member.

At the same time they were so freely discursive concern-

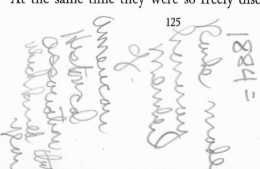

ing what they considered their indebtedness to their bodily remote but spiritually close associate that their thought on this score can be confidently summed up in two co-ordinated statements. The first of these affirmed that henceforth history was to be based solely on original documents, that is, on documents contemporary with the event described, but, and the point is crucial, only after such documents had been subjected to a critical examination covering their authenticity, origin, authorship, and bias. With the documents stripped by this procedure of obscuring ingredients and cut down to their essential factual core, the second statement came into play. This statement, no longer analytical but compositional in character, prescribed the cool, objective fitting together of the assembled mass of basic facts into the true and indisputable picture of the past event. This crowning labor Ranke himself had defined in the famous phrase *wie es eigentlich gewesen.* In spite of its having lost its freshness through continued exorcistic repetition, it cannot be passed over because it remains the most effective statement of its author's belief that by the pursuit of his method the historian is able to recover the past event as it actually occurred.

We may entertain no doubt that the American historians with practical unanimity took over the new method as summarized in the foregoing terms. Not till the close of the century was any doubt voiced as to the entire adequacy of Ranke's guidance for his American adherents. By that time the recently awakened interest in economic developments and in the closely related social transformation had gained so much vigor that the too exclusive concentration of the German leader on data of a purely political nature was noted as a defect of scope. Then in the early decades of the twentieth century the critical chorus gained both volume and intensity and aimed its shafts no longer merely at the failure to take account of material of steadily increasing urgence—material belonging to such newly developed fields as economics, sociology, and psychology—but also at some suspected defects of the method's compositional feature. There was no denying that while the American historians in their vast majority continued to cling to the guiding principles to which they had become committed, the image of their admired exemplar had begun to lose some of its original glow. When in these altered circumstances Charles A. Beard, speaking in 1933 with the ex cathedra authority of a president of the American Historical Association, undertook definitely to terminate the Rankean ascendancy, it seemed, at least to a like-minded group of listeners, that they had witnessed the ejection of their honorary member from the niche to which he had been enthusiastically elevated a half-century before.

Beard's presidential address contains so much matter of the greatest theoretical importance that it calls for detailed consideration. But before undertaking it, let us note that his repudiation of Ranke and what he stood for won the approval of no more than a fraction of his colleagues. A resolute majority held to the established faith, firmly refusing to be swept off their feet by a quasi-official ban skilfully compounded of argument and mockery. At the very next, the 1934, meeting of the association, Professor Theodore Clarke Smith made himself the spokesman of the stalwart majority and in a paper, entitled "The Writing of American History," took angry exception to Beard's radical pronouncement. In effective support of his conservative position he

Beards attack of idea (...predicts as they actually happened)

pointed with unconcealed pride to the notable harvest gathered by American historians during the preceding half-century through pursuit of the method which, while originating in Germany, had demonstrably become the accredited method of the historical profession throughout the world.

It must not be supposed that in consequence of the blows exchanged between Beard and Smith the American historians were split into two bitterly warring factions. Theoretical discussion has never been a prime interest with any of our American learned groups, and the debate over Beard's provocative attack has remained within the strictly gentlemanly bounds observed by native scholarship from the beginning. Nevertheless, as a break or attempted break from an accepted faith and practice it possesses a significance that calls for a presentation of at least its essential elements. Let it be said at once that Beard has no quarrel with what we have laid down as the first of the two Rankean master principles. His disclaimer is exclusively aimed at the second or compositional directive, the much bandied *wie es eigentlich gewesen.* Consider, says Beard, the bewildering totality of facts from which the historian undertakes to shape the picture of the past. His first view of them is a surging chaos, which he then attempts to reduce to some kind of order and intelligibility by a process of selection. In this operation he is unavoidably guided by certain subjective criteria inherent in his personality and often so deeply buried that they hardly, if at all, rise to the level of consciousness. Ranke's own case provides a convincing demonstration of this never failing personal entanglement. His theory called for an objective, that is, a strictly detached putting-together of the ascertained facts in order to arrive at the true image of the past; but since he was a man living in a definite environment at a particular moment of time, his mind and outlook necessarily reflected these limitations. In religion a believing Lutheran Christian, in politics a devoted subject of the Prussian monarchy, he was cast in a narrow conservative mold in a period of European civilization profoundly disturbed by the continuing radical agitation released by the French Revolution. By nature an unusually calm and contained spirit, he may be assumed to have been less influenced by his inherited attachments than historians in general are likely to be; but it is, of course, inescapable that he was to a measurable degree affected by them and that he tinged his claimed objective findings with a subjective bias.

Having explained why it is that the past does not lend itself to the objective presentation held by Ranke to be imperative, Beard goes on to reject the view implicit in the Rankean postulate that the past somehow persists in the depths of time, awaiting like the Sleeping Beauty of the fairy tale the advent of her bespectacled, seminar-trained deliverer. This view to Beard is pure illusion—an illusion already disposed of by the admitted subjective nature of historical composition and scattered beyond hope of recovery by the circumstance that, though the historian's earliest and continuing concern is with a frightening multitude of petty facts, he gives them, through considered reflection, that is, by an act of thought, a coherence and pattern not native to them.

With this final twist to his view of the nature of historical composition Beard takes his stand at the side of Benedetto Croce, Italian philosopher and leading historical theorist. When after the usual elucidative flourishes Croce at last formulates his answer to the query What is history? he replies succinctly: "History is contemporary thought about the past." Let it be pointed out at once that there is an ambiguity about this compact statement which may not be evaded. For even if "contemporary thought" be accepted as the act immediately preceding composition, is it at liberty to picture the past to suit its subjective whim, or must it submit to the guidance of the particular facts assembled and screened by documentary research? And since it is the second or alternative choice which will imperatively impose itself, does it not follow that "contemporary thought" cannot escape the necessity of accommodating itself to Ranke's critical method?

Under the head of history in general Beard is at pains to distinguish among the many diversified meanings of the term. He identifies history in its broadest sense as "past actuality" and embraces within it everything that has been done, said, felt, and thought since the beginning of man's presence on earth. However, it is not in this all-embracing sense but in the narrow meaning of composition that history figures in common usage. Owing to every composed work's origin in thought and owing, further, to the shifting nature of thought from age to age, each generation insists on recasting the history it has received from its predecessor. While this constant reshaping of the past has long been noticed, it has not been utilized, at least not to the full extent of its significance, as evidence against the view of the past as objective, inalterable truth.

In closing his paper, Beard enlarged his inquiry to embrace a number of theoretical considerations not strictly stemming from the Ranke problem. One of these deals with mental background and asserts that every history deserving the name rests on a philosophy. Of the two basic philosophies enjoying the greatest present-day vogue, the older goes back to the eighteenth century and is optimistically tinged with that century's faith in reason and with its faith in the amazing achievements of the natural sciences, hailed by reason as reason's indisputable fruit. Reduced to philosophical terms, this faith holds that mankind is slowly moving on an upward gradient to a more ideal order. Although the twentieth century with its two devastating wars of world scope has gravely dimmed the optimism which is the vital spark of this outlook, it still underlies a large proportion of histories of the most recent date.

The most vigorous rival philosophy is of nineteenth-century origin. Its author is Karl Marx, and it sailed under the flag of "socialism." Its basic contention is the conflict of social classes, which will unhappily continue until capitalism and private property are abolished and the state has taken over the means of production and distribution. While the historian is not obliged to resort to one or the other of these two philosophies in most common use, he must resort to a philosophy of some kind if he wishes to give his work the coherence and order indispensable to making it an intelligible communication. In the case of Ranke, Beard, in a casual manner, and Croce, his theoretical guide and ally, more definitely, charge that the German master lacks a philosophy. While in the light of the indicated process of historical composition this could not possibly be true, it carries the limited truth that Ranke accepted neither the eighteenth-century "progress" nor the nineteenth-century "socialist" conception of the development of mankind. As a deeply religious man Ranke held it to be high presumption to forecast a future for mankind on the basis of purely secular considerations. In his view the future rests with God, who is forever inscrutable. While this attitude will be unacceptable to followers of either of the above-named schools of thought, which are of an essentially identical, that is, a rationalist, origin, nonetheless it is a philosophy, the ancient and venerable philosophy, in fact, that underlies Christianity. We shall return to this issue later on.

The twentieth-century decline of Ranke's authority in the United States was paralleled by its decline in his own country, Germany. While the native diminution may be attributed in part to the same agencies as those operative across the Atlantic, an influence of an entirely different nature made itself felt which, though nameless at the time, was afterward labeled *Historismus*. This was a freshly coined word translatable by the equally freshly coined English word, "historicism." According to Heussi[1] the word did not appear in print till around the year 1900, when it took shape as an attempted definition of the spirit of German history writing of that period. The statement was not wholly acceptable to Troeltsch[2] and Meinecke,[3] who may be selected as figuring most prominently with Heussi in the lively discussion over *Historismus* which stirred German historical circles. While there was agreement among the debaters on the essentials of the issue, there were differences on details, quite the most important stemming from Meinecke. Agreeing that the word made the late appearance noted by Heussi, Meinecke insisted that the practice represented by the word

1. Karl Heussi, *Die Krisis des Historismus* (Tübingen, 1932).
2. Ernst Troeltsch, *Der Historismus und seine Probleme* (1922).
3. Friedrich Meinecke, *Die Entstehung des Historismus* (2 vols., 1936).

originated over a hundred years earlier and, slowly gathering strength, reached maturity during the life of Ranke, to whom it then largely owed its fulfilment and ascendancy.

For Troeltsch and Meinecke, with their deeper perspective than Heussi, historicism arose as a normal human reaction to the dominant rationalism of the eighteenth century and in its earliest manifestations was identical with the Romantic movement. This famous outlook found eager propagators in every country of Europe and by the beginning of the nineteenth century boasted a range as wide as Western civilization. Conspicuous among its early German champions were Winckelmann, Lessing, Moeser, Herder, and Goethe. During Ranke's impressionable youth romanticism constituted his country's ruling intellectual atmosphere, and this was further strengthened by the leading political event of that period, the overthrow of Napoleon Bonaparte. For to the Romantics the emperor was the last and most fearful expression of the rationalism that had brought on the French Revolution. The political counterpart of the total Romantic mood was therefore a violent reaction in favor of the many institutions, particularly the monarchy and the church, which the Revolution had attacked as outmoded historical lumber.

If we now note that through birth and inheritance Ranke's religious allegiance was to the Lutheran church and his political allegiance to the cause of monarchy, we are prepared to understand that his immediate instinctive attitude toward the issues raised by rationalism was anti-revolutionary. However, familiar as a historian with the past development of mankind, he felt impelled to fortify his spontaneous position with examples and arguments drawn from recorded human experience. Eighteenth-century rationalism had claimed universal validity for its principles and, thus inspired, had loftily rejected the widely diverse laws, customs, and institutions handed down from an irrational past. It was in protest against this systematic leveling of cherished earthborn diversities that romanticism had come to life, and it was through the expression Ranke gave to the protest in the domain of government that he became a leading propagator of historicism.

On seeking to learn more precisely what it was that Ranke contributed to the shaping of historicism, we must, since this is a theoretical issue, turn first to such theoretical statements as he himself may have delivered. Surprising though it may seem at first, we learn that, given over to creative historical production, he felt so little inclined to spin theories about his work that his efforts in this department reduce themselves pretty much to a single brief article. This is his *Politisches Gespräch* or "Dialogue on Politics,"[4] which he contributed in 1836 to the *Historisch-politische Zeitschrift,* a government-supported magazine of which he was the editor. The central purpose of the article was unmistakably the defense of the Prussian monarchy against the agitation of German liberal circles influenced by English and French thought in favor of a modification of Prussian absolutism through the adoption of a constitution. Ranke rests his defense on the assertion that not only Prussia but every state possesses a peculiar self-developing germ or genius and that, thus endowed, it is a living, individual entity. Far from

4. Published in *Sämmtliche Werke,* Vols. XLIX–L, ed. Alfred Dove (1887); translated as "Dialogue on Politics" in T. H. von Laue's *Leopold Ranke: The Formative Years* (Princeton: Princeton University Press, 1950).

admitting that conflict must follow from the juxtaposition of numerous organizational diversities, he chooses to enlarge on the enrichment of life resulting from the coexistence of systems, each of which has the merit of being a spontaneous natural growth. Here, if anywhere, we touch on the origin and primary meaning of historicism: it offered as the replacement of the revolutionary appeal to reason the evolutionary appeal to history.

From the claim of an inviolable personality made for Prussia (and by implication for every other state) certain deductions flowed which, though but rarely expressly touched on by Ranke with his distaste for doctrinal excursions, have nonetheless received abundant interlinear expression in his histories. In one and all of his works he accepted, without expressly expounding his position, the right of war as an instrument of policy. While as a good Christian he could not glory in war for its own sake and did not do so, yet, by upholding war as a legitimate means of defense from attack, he in effect abandoned such religious scruples as he may originally have had. For every state on declaring war follows the practice of asserting with hysterical clamor that, regardless of contrary appearances, it is actually only defending itself against an attack either already in progress or about to be launched. All wars are represented by their participants as defensive wars.

Closely connected with his acceptance of defensive war was his consistent support of what he called the *Primat der Aussenpolitik,* a principle according to which governments were bound, for the imperative reason of self-preservation, to give primary consideration to foreign affairs. States like England and France, however, owing no doubt to their living under a parliamentary dispensation which put them under the immediate pressure of public opinion, were often disposed to be swayed by domestic rather than by foreign considerations. It may therefore be concluded that Ranke's view of the priority to be unfailingly conceded to foreign affairs derived from his reading of Prussian history and that by this preference, which he consistently maintained, he lent his support to the cause of continuing absolutism.

It should not for a moment be supposed that Ranke was an embattled champion of these views. He never departed from the quiet, tolerant manner of expression that was native to him and that he had adopted from the time of his earliest attempt at authorship as the tone appropriate to historical exposition. But steadfast attachment to an undeviating line of thought through a life of patriarchal longevity marked by an unrivaled number of works of universally recognized merit did more toward spreading and confirming the outstanding features of his outlook than could possibly have resulted from an ever ready panoplied descent into the arena. Even before he had reached his middle years, he found himself lifted to a throne he had not sought and credited with a wisdom he never claimed. It followed that his thinking on war, on the primacy of foreign affairs, and on Prussia as a unique political creation became to a remarkable degree the treasured possession not only of his German professional associates but also of the whole German intelligentsia.

The total effect of these particularities of German political thinking opened a rift which under the mounting pressure of the nineteenth-century rivalry among the European powers widened to an unbridgeable chasm between Prussia-Germany, on the one hand, and England and France, the leading powers of the West, on the other. This was a threat ready to develop into the disruption of Western civilization. And this is precisely what happened in the following, the twentieth century in the course of two monstrous wars that sucked practically all the states bordering on the Atlantic and Pacific oceans into the vortex and thus achieved a world-wide scope.

The first of these world clashes ended with the defeat of Prussia-Germany and the replacement of the discredited monarchy of the Hohenzollerns with a democratic republic. It represented an attempted accommodation to the political system of the victor powers; but, unfortunately, and largely because it was a product of military defeat and national shame, it failed to take root in the German soul. There were too many anti-republican groups which, although professing distinct and individual views, by a continued and inflamed agitation on behalf of Germany's traditional separateness and asserted separate destiny, were ready to be fused into an irresistible anti-republican mass. Under a demagogue endowed with such hypnotic power as has repeatedly in the course of history produced fanatic mob action, there followed in due time the destruction of the experimental republic and the elevation of the triumphant demagogue to the dizzy and terrifying height of a dictator. Therewith we broach the Hitler episode, which, like every similar explosion in the human record, will on close examination be found to have been the resultant of innumerable coincidental forces but which, in final analysis, is mainly referable to the divergent political line, in both theory and practice, taken by Prussia-Germany in the general European reconstruction following the overthrow of Napoleon Bonaparte.

The despair that seized the population on the crushing defeat of the Hitler regime in World War II inevitably produced a violent reaction against all the postulates on which
the regime rested. Some of these, as, for instance, its racial
and anti-Semitic theories, were the special contributions of
Hitler's distorted mind; but others, more particularly those
of a political nature, went straight back to dominant German
thought, the seedbed of which was the Romantic movement.
But since romanticism, politically viewed, had taken shape
as historicism, it followed that the sharp reaction produced
by annihilative defeat induced a review of the constitutive
elements of historicism, at least by that segment of the historians and the general public elastic enough to adjust its
thinking to the disruptive consequences of a national earth-
quake. Since Ranke was generally acclaimed as the father of
historicism, his reputation has suffered a commensurate decline which simple-minded people, whose mental myopia
takes in only the more obvious aspects of change, interpreted
as total eclipse.

Since this writer regards the opinion that Ranke should
be consigned to the limbo of dead historians as a gross mis-
judgment, he proposes to undertake a re-examination of his
work with the purpose of setting forth its leading characteristics and evaluating the total achievement.

Although young Ranke's studies at the University of Leipzig, where he obtained the Doctor's degree in 1817, prepared
him for a career in classical philology and literature, he had
no sooner received a teaching appointment from the Prussian
government to the high school (*gymnasium*) in the provincial town of Frankfort on the Oder than his interest be-

gan to swing to classical history and thence to history in general. Owing to a feeling for authenticity, he was not long in arriving at the conclusion that history must be constructed from its true, that is, from strictly contemporary sources. It was in 1824, when he was twenty-nine years old, that he first drew professional attention to this demand by showing that Guicciardini in his *La Storia d'Italia* had to a large degree extracted his factual substance from feeble, secondary sources. This work had long enjoyed an immense reputation as marking the emergence of a modern as distinct from a medieval type of historical writing. Since it had never occurred to anyone to examine it in respect to its constituent elements, Ranke's demonstration of its insecure base created a professional sensation.

The critique of Guicciardini was the first gun fired by Ranke in a lifelong campaign to win for history the best attainable factual underpinning through a searching preliminary analysis of the available source material. This campaign was supplemented by an action calling attention to the variety of existing sources and their places of deposit. His enthusiasm for these repositories drew much of its fervor from his having hit by chance on an invaluable collection of accounts contemporary with the events described, the Venetian *relazioni*. These were reports sent to the government of Venice by its ambassadors, unquestionably the most keen-witted observers of the political scene to be found within the compass of Europe at the beginning of the modern period. Copies of some of these reports had found their way to German libraries and archives, where the browsing Ranke, on discovering them, was quick to perceive their unrivaled fulness and precision.

On the heels of his revelation of Guicciardini's slipshod procedure the young scholar was called to the University of Berlin to a position approximately corresponding to that of an American assistant professor; and three years later he was awarded a Prussian state fellowship for study among Italian archives, more particularly at Venice, the locus of that priceless treasury, the *relazioni*. Pausing on his southward journey for some months at Vienna, he turned his stay into a highly rewarding experience by composing from the oral communications of a Serb refugee the vivid story of the recently suppressed revolt of the Serbs against the dominion of the sultan. In October, 1828, he entered Italy, and there, in that land of medieval and Renaissance culture, during the next three years he gleaned with never flagging zest among the archives an immense mass of documentary material, selecting his documents always with an eye to future creative production. This he began promptly on his return to Germany and thereafter pursued with a diligence and devotion which enabled him to produce a body of works poured out in a steady stream throughout a vigorous manhood and a patriarchal old age. It is a well-known fact but so astonishing as to deserve ever to be recalled to mind that he had passed his eightieth birthday when he undertook the most ambitious enterprise of his career, the *Weltgeschichte,* which, overtaken by death, he left unfinished.

Such is the vastness of this long-lived scholar's output that his *Sämmtliche Werke* run to a total of fifty-four volumes. Although all of them are relevant for the present survey, it will promote our deeper understanding if, instead of ranging over the whole wide prospect, we direct our attention in the main to those works which have been generally accepted as providing the solid basis of his reputation. These are, in the order of their appearance, *The Ottoman and Spanish Empires in the Sixteenth and Seventeenth Centuries, The History of the Popes of Rome in the Sixteenth and Seventeenth Centuries, The History of the Reformation in Germany, The Civil Wars and Monarchy in France in the Sixteenth and Seventeenth Centuries,* and *A History of England Principally in the Seventeenth Century.* The list will at once disclose that the author made the sixteenth and seventeenth centuries his field of special interest. But in order to concede his admission to the select company of historians who have survived their mortal term he must have succeeded in illuminating the broad era of his choice. On this as yet unsettled issue of his survival the eclipse of his authority, resulting from his part in developing the afterward repudiated movement of historicism, has no bearing, for the above-listed works belong, one and all, to a period of Western civilization when the tension between rationalism and romanticism, which, as we have shown, gave birth to historicism, had not yet arisen. In the period which Ranke chose to illuminate, rationalism was experiencing no more than its earliest birth pangs, while romanticism was still slumbering, awaiting its hour, in the womb of time. The central dominating theme of the centuries to which our author's leading works belong was the Catholic-Protestant conflict. Ranke's avowed Lutheranism did not render him incapable of maintaining a just balance regarding the religious struggle, since not only had its onetime fury spent itself by the time he wrote but his private thinking had progressed beyond mere toleration to a deep respect for every variety of honest religious belief. Only a Catholic or Protestant extremist will refuse to agree that in respect to the religious strife he depicted he dwelt consistently above the battle.

Besides this rare fair-mindedness the listed works boast the notable distinction of constituting, by the survey they make of the countries chiefly concerned with the Reformation and Counter Reformation, a comprehensive history of the Europe of that age. This result accorded with a breadth of view that had characterized Ranke from the beginning. By reason thereof he became the first secular writer consistently to stress the essential unity of western Europe, in spite of the separate and contentious sovereign states of which it was composed. Never for a moment did he fail to take account of the uninterrupted interaction of the separate sovereignties on the religious, political, material, and moral level. Yet significant as this cultural nexus was, it was unrepresented by any officially established organ. However, since it did in fact exist, it had to be given a name; it thus figured in Ranke's narrative as the "system of European states." It was a phrase too narrowly political to win prolonged acceptance, and it was gradually superseded by the more expressive, because more inclusive, term "Western civilization." While this was a natural and wholesome expansion of Ranke's concept, it undebatably covered the same phenomenon. Consequently it may fairly be claimed that to his ranging mind belongs the honor of having shown that, while separate and distinct histories of the component nations of Europe may and will continue to be written, they will be lacking in due perspective and a desirable maturity of thought, unless they are firmly set in the total European context. In short, the thesis underlying the histories of Ranke has won universal recognition—politically divided Europe was culturally one.

The universalizing tendency of Ranke's thinking sprang unquestionably from his Christian faith, since in the manner of a true believer he regarded all the peoples of the earth, and in a very special sense the Christian peoples of Europe, as dwelling under God's hand. It followed that he left the resolution of man's unceasing struggle toward a higher order of living to the divine Father. Such humility put him out of touch with the major portion of his fellow craftsmen, who, as previously indicated, organized their histories under either a rationalist or a socialist concept. Since this majority accepted the guidance of a recently achieved purely secular doctrine, they resented Ranke's position as an outmoded childish act of faith unworthy of a liberated intelligence. But were the rival versions of man's goal as indisputably deducible from the historical record as their proponents claimed they were? It would certainly not seem so to this writer, to whom it appears that they rested in the last analysis on a postulate as distinctly constituting an act of faith as Ranke's divine postulate. The only admissible ground for claiming the superiority of these two still current rationalist and socialist projections of man's future over Ranke's Christian projection would be that, while in better accord with the facts of man's past development, they hold out the prospect of a richer development for mankind. But that is by no means the case, since they sketch a future existence shut within the narrow bounds of a highly debatable intellectual concept. As against this contracted world Ranke's divine concept unfolds an open road into an unbounded region inviting inexhaustible exploration. It is the identical terra incognita toward which the sages of our race from the earliest days have searchingly turned their gaze without discovering its

143

ultimate limit or true significance. *Ignoramus,* they concluded, we do not know. In view of their humility before an unfathomed mystery, may we not ask what compulsive reason there is to believe that latter-day thinkers—call them sages if you will—of the order of Jeremy Bentham and Karl Marx have at long last penetrated the veil of our ignorance?

That God was the shaper of man's lot on earth was already so settled a conviction of the young high-school teacher of provincial Frankfort that his first book was fairly saturated with it. This was *The History of the Romanic and Germanic Peoples from 1494 to 1514.* It was published in 1824, before he was called to Berlin, and may be regarded as an introductory work announcing the plan for expounding the European development of the sixteenth and seventeenth centuries, to which he then devoted the immediately succeeding decades of his life. That he was at the time a mere beginner, a tyro, is revealed by both the style and the matter of his book and, most convincingly, by the crudely naïve way he has God intervene in human affairs. As a man with a fund of natural good taste he quickly cured himself of this simpleminded procedure, and, although his faith in God's direction remained unchanged, he thenceforth kept it out of his narrative in this obvious form.

By the time he began the great series on which his fame mainly rests he had reached the conclusion that the immediately operative and at the same time measurably calculable agency in human affairs is ideas. While he deals with ideas on the strictly human level which their rational treatment demands, he holds that they are products of the spirit stemming, in last analysis, from the divine Creator. They are therefore in Ranke's view the means by which the Creator

144

carries out his purposes; but since they exercise rule over the minds of men and produce the conflicts among them which effect the onward movement of society, they permit a presentation of human affairs which, while keeping the person of God out of the picture, points nevertheless to his unmistakable direction. So important is the role of ideas throughout Ranke's history writing that there is no leading work of his in which he is not moved, however briefly, to set it forth. In *The History of the Popes,* for instance, he declares categorically that it is ideas that are the cause of historical change ("Die Ideen welche die Dinge bewegen"); and in *The History of the Reformation in Germany* he speaks almost rhapsodically of "the fullness of the spiritual life God breathes upon the human race." In another passage of the same book he insists that ideas determine every human situation, and he goes on to say of their appearance and disappearance, their birth and decay: "For a time they are beneficent and life-giving, new creations arise under their breath. However, nothing on earth achieves completion, nothing is immortal. When the time is ripe new spiritual purposes spring from the decay of their predecessors. Thus it is that God's design fulfills itself" ("Das sind die Geschicke Gottes in der Welt").

Since Ranke was ruled by this undeviating faith, what were his chances of satisfying the cool objectivity which he demanded as a self-imposed law of the writer of histories? Very small indeed, we are bound to conclude. In point of fact, his exposition of events was as far removed from perfect objectivity as has always been and must inescapably be the exposition of every historian endowed with a distinct soul and character. He was a religious man possessed as only a religious man can be of a deep inner harmony, and this harmony set a corresponding imprint on his Christianity, causing him to shed a mild, pervasive optimism over all his work. Although historical Christian teaching presented God sometimes as a vengeful, sometimes as a loving, deity, for Ranke he was always a God of love. Unconsciously yielding to this temperamental bias, he was moved to ignore or at least lightly to pass over the more cruel and disturbing aspects of the human scene. While he could not and did not suppress the wars into which the fierce rivalries of the European powers periodically exploded, he was disinclined to concern himself with their details and particularly with their attendant barbarities. And when it came to such infamous horrors as the Peasant War in Germany and the purge of St. Bartholomew in France, which many of his less sensitive confreres through the ages have ridden as their prancing battle horses, he was pleased to dispose of them in a cool, abbreviated account free from all emotional overtones.

It would therefore appear that in his demand for objectivity as well as in the related demand to recover the past event *wie es eigentlich gewesen,* Ranke fell into a certain self-deception. Or did he? For nowhere does he speak of these paired desiderata as absolutes, and, alert as he was to human shortcomings, he cannot possibly have believed that they were realizable in an absolute sense. It is a fact that while he originated the famous phrase, it was not he but his blind followers who made a slogan of it. It is therefore entirely reasonable to conclude that he was content to set forth the two related demands as general aims; and as general aims they possess an unchallengeable validity. Freely admitting the inability of the historian either to restore the exact image of the past or to practice a mindless objectivity, we may yet insist that he aims at a desirable goal when he strives to get as close to a given past event as the evidence permits in order to set it forth undistorted by at least his grosser prejudices.

Whoever lovingly concerns himself with Ranke's writings will not be long in discovering that the purpose which most steadily animated him was, in Von Laue's luminous words, "the happy cognition of each unique event in the story of man." He was not at pains to distinguish among events as more or less important or to distinguish among epochs according to a hierarchy of values. In the addresses held at Berchtesgaden (1854) he delivered himself of a crucial statement on this point: "I am committed to the view that every epoch stands in an immediate relation to God and that its value does not depend on what it produces but simply on its existence." It is in strict keeping with these words to assume that he strove to take toward the occurrences on our globe the imagined position of the Creator, who, tossing them off in unbroken succession, rates them as equally good. It is this attitude that explains why the generally held "progress" theory of eighteenth- and nineteenth-century rationalism had no lure for him. He might agree that there had been "progress" in the limited sense of a vast increase of material goods, but he could not bring himself to admit that there was a clearly traceable line of advance which gave invincible assurance of the raising of our human lot to a higher potential. His repeatedly expressed deliberate opinion was that world history had no humanly recognizable goal. Instead of letting himself be dejected and saddened by this uncertainty, he accepted it with the quiet rejoicing befitting a believer

147

who was content not presumptuously to forestall God's unfathomed purposes.

Therewith we have arrived at the question of what the particular satisfaction may have been that Ranke drew from the
pursuit of history, since it was not the usual one of throwing
such light as the latest increase of knowledge had made
available on man's ceaseless struggle. The answer from
which there is no escape is so far removed from present-day
sympathies and understanding that the pen hesitates to set
it down. Only if we once more recall that, in spite of the
heaped conquests of reason and its handmaid science, the
world remained an unresolved mystery for Ranke, will we
be prepared to come to terms with the declaration that, in
addition to the readily understandable pleasure associated
with his beloved daily labors, he received ever renewed and
inexhaustible delight from the aesthetic contemplation of
the pictured events his research placed before his eyes. The
statement reveals an element in this historian which has
been rather generally overlooked, especially in the United
States. Ranke was not merely a scholar, he was also that
much rarer thing, an artist, and it was to his artistic gift that
he owed the vivacity that endowed his work with its in-
vigorating pulse beat. Among his frequent references to the
roles of scholarship and artistry in the writing of history one
of the most explicit is to be found in *A History of France*:
"The task of the historian is both literary and scholarly:
history is both art and science. It must satisfy the demands
of criticism and scholarship . . . and simultaneously provide
the cultured reader with the same enjoyment he derives
from the most acceptable literary production."

This view of his activity imposed the obligation on him

of keeping art and scholarship in an even balance, and this was not always easy. By official status he was a university professor who conducted a famous seminar for the training of professionally minded students. When not engaged in teaching, he was a closet-scholar so happily given to his daily stint of work that he adopted as his personal motto the clipped phrase: *labor ipse voluptas.* Steeped in this bookish atmosphere, he inevitably succumbed at times, especially after age had begun to bank his youthful fires, to the passion of gathering knowledge for its own sake and thereby burdening his text with more matter than its artistic form would support. That this imbalance may at least in part be attributed to his advancing years is borne out by the fact that his relatively late French and English histories suffer from it much more than the earlier works. But no one will maintain that on that account these later, occasionally overstuffed productions are not in the category of his leading works. And how can the theory of a decline of workmanship running parallel to his descending years be successfully maintained when the *Weltgeschichte,* which he did not attack till his middle eighties, is floated on an energy which the lustiest youth might envy?

No, it will not do to lay his unfortunate occasional departures from the desirable fusion of learning and art to his waxing years, at least not exclusively. For it will not escape the attentive reader that, whenever the accumulations of Ranke the scholar threaten to extinguish the light shed by Ranke the artist, the blight befalls in the realm of diplomacy. It is this circumstance that accounts for his rating by one school of his latter-day detractors as essentially a diplomatic historian. While this is undebatably a one-sided judgment, it must be admitted that he brought it on himself by his excessive regard for sovereign states and their contentious dealings with one another through their accredited diplomatic representatives.

We pointed out in an earlier section of this essay that Ranke was at the peak of his production at a time antecedent to the development of many of the present-day ancillary branches of history, such as economic and social history, and that consequently his work, lacking the support of these later elaborations, has for contemporary ears something of an antiquated flavor. However, if the complaint is justified that he carried his eager tracings of the minute and boresome shifts of official government opinion too far for the taste of the living generation, he must be defended against the charge of ignoring the much more important human societies on which the governments rested and by which they lived. Beginning with his first masterwork and continuing without exception through all its successors, he made it a practice to set forth all those aspects of the society under review for which he found material in the sources at his command. In *The History of the Popes,* for instance, he presents an exposition of the papal finances that leaves nothing to be desired by way of income and outgo figures and the attendant administrative manipulations. Then, on taking up the Italian culture of the Counter Reformation at its peak around the year 1600, he shows how it completely reversed all the intellectual and artistic tendencies of the preceding age of the Renaissance. This startling about-face he follows up with a detailed view of the realms of literature, art, and science, displaying an insight and delicate perception that no present-day writer armed with the latest equipment of graphs and statistics is likely to surpass or even to rival.

If our age makes more of economics than of culture, that is a preference that is readily explained in the light of twentieth-century developments; but let no one say that Ranke in analyzing the culture of the Counter Reformation performed a work of supererogation and that his superb review does not of itself suffice to cancel the slur that he was a man of an exclusively diplomatic outlook. Furthermore, since he does not fail to illuminate the non-political aspects of all the other societies with which he deals, the German, the French, the English, with similarly penetrating expositions in the social and cultural fields, we are bound to conclude that, in spite of their disproportionately large diplomatic ingredient, his histories cover an equally interesting, though not an identical, range as works of our more broadly curious and more widely informed age.

Since Ranke's scholarly reputation dates from the critical method with which he made his professional debut and since his reputation is still unimpaired so far as his treatment of sources is concerned, it remains to have a look at his literary merits. If the dictum attributed to Buffon is true—*le style c'est l'homme*—Ranke must have been endowed at his birth with a stylistic gift. But that does not mean that he was not moved to refine it by constant practice until it had developed into an elastic medium suited to the rendering of many varieties of mood and intention. His greatest achievement was the mastery of a direct, uncomplicated, easily flowing narrative style admirably accommodated to the main content of his works. So adeptly is this narrative manner employed that each sentence glows with an inner spark and the story the sentence chain unfolds comes vividly to life. He was less successful with drama than narration because its high tension was not congenial to his nature. His diction is rich and varied and his sentence structure particularly noteworthy, since the German tradition favored the serpentining sentence so hampered with dependent clauses that its vital movement was brought to a dead stop before its message had been delivered. Let us consider by way of illustration of his usual form of presentation the relatively uneventful chapter in *The History of the Reformation in Germany* which treats of Luther's growing estrangement from the Roman church in the period between the posting of the ninety-five theses and his appearance before the Diet at Worms. No one, it seems to this writer, can fail to be impressed with the sparkle investing the many small separate incidents whose cumulative power carries the reader onward to the famous incident before the emperor. Arrived, however, at this scene of high-keyed drama, he characteristically fails to realize its inherent possibilities.

To break his narrative with a change of pace and matter Ranke adopted the practice of drawing the portrait of the outstanding figures of his tale. Since he wrote before the advent of modern psychology, he was unable to take advantage of the insight it provides into the subconscious life and the hidden complexes which play so large a part in human conduct. On this account his portraiture has in recent years occasionally been rated as superficial and outmoded. Valid or not, such strictures do not diminish by a shade the vitality which invests the Ranke portrait gallery. Let us concentrate for a moment on the portrait of Paul III in the first volume of *The History of the Popes*. Paul III was the pope who marked the transition from the outlook of the Renaissance to the outlook of the Counter Reformation, and his unconscious shuttling from one to the other of these contrasted periods is perfectly realized in what came to be Ranke's habitual portraitizing manner. This may be characterized as peculiarly suited to the historian, for, essentially pragmatic and documentary, it consisted in listing the significant experiences of the subject's life interspersed with revealing utterances by himself and comments on him by eyewitnesses and contemporaries. The success of the method depends upon wise selection and requires a broad cultural prospect to employ effectively.

Since a continued lively interest in the mind and heart of an author is likely to awaken a desire to know something of his physical appearance, we note that Ranke was a smallish man with a disproportionately large head. After his death former students recalled different aspects of his person. Giesebrecht, a famous medievalist in his day, recorded the penetrating glance of the master's large blue eyes and the flowing dark hair that framed his face. Gregorovius, a very casual acquaintance, reports the slight scholar's hump that put in an appearance on the threshold of old age. By general agreement he was not a good lecturer and owed the impression that made him unforgettable to his large body of advanced students to the masterful conduct of his seminar. Two distinguished Americans, W. W. Story and Henry Adams, have left a very unfavorable report of his platform manner and appearance.

In closing, let us frankly face the question of Ranke's survival. He has already outlived his death for over half a century, although recently, as we have seen, his reputation has visibly paled. Fifty years is not much more than a human generation, but not many historians have lived on even so long as that. History in general would seem to be a form of literature hardly less ephemeral than journalism. Only a very select number of its practitioners have achieved immortality, and of this number it may be said without hesitation that in every instance they owed their distinction to the fruitful marriage they effected between scholarship and art. Neither of these factors takes precedence over the other; it is the successfully achieved balance that produces the endurance of the finished work.

While Ranke by his own confession strove to do justice to this double demand, he did at times, especially when in his later years he had become too rutted in his workday world, let scholarship run away with his art. There can be no question that the histories reflecting the greatest harmony of style and matter are Ranke's earliest large-scale works, *The History of the Popes* and *The History of the Reformation in Germany*. It is revealing in this connection that these two, and these alone, have won a general popularity. The French and English histories, apart from their excessive diplomatic baggage, are too long spun out. It would be a distinct service if some sympathetic spirit would reduce them to half their size by judicious cutting. It is on these four works that the issue of his survival principally turns. While it is plain that the time is not yet ripe for a final verdict, it is fairly safe to place him, in view of his total contributions in his field and his extraordinary influence in his day on his fellow craftsmen, at the head of the historians of the nineteenth century.

BIBLIOGRAPHICAL NOTE

Ranke's *Sämmtliche Werke* were published in 1867–81 in fifty-four volumes. There are English translations of *The History of the Popes, The History of the Reformation in Germany, The Civil Wars and Monarchy in France in the Sixteenth and Seventeenth Centuries, The History of England Principally in the Seventeenth Century;* also of some minor works, such as *A History of Servia and the Servian Revolution.*

HENRY ADAMS

Achievement and Defeat

Since his death in 1918 Henry Adams has been acclaimed by
an ever widening circle of Americans both as his country's
leading historian and as perhaps the most complete expression in his day of its unfolding culture. However, it is impossible to rest content with the statement of his achievement in these simple terms, since to do so would be to ignore
the enormous complexities of mind and character that have
made him one of the most enigmatic personages of our national story. While it is the present writer's intention to
make these complexities the chief feature of this essay, it will
facilitate understanding to anticipate the later elaboration
by a short preliminary survey of the development of the interests that successively engaged Adams' attention.

Beginning life as a member of the most famous family of

157

his native Boston, he both consciously and unconsciously absorbed mental and moral traits which, in spite of his later determined effort to reduce them and even shake them off entirely, kept a firm grip on him to the end of his days. The earliest of these traits to assert itself was the urge to win distinction and an appropriate post of power by the public service which had carried his great-grandfather and his grandfather to the presidency of the United States and had won for his father the key embassy at London in the critical period of the Civil War. This earliest purpose may be said to have been his chief directive until it was smothered by a deep disgust with politics generated by his viewing at close quarters in Washington the monstrous corruption of the Grant administration.

If we accept his hopes for a public career and their bitter disappointment as defining the first stage of his development, the second stage began with a sharp break marked by his acceptance in 1870, at the age of thirty-two, of a professorship in history at Harvard College. Nothing in his previous training had prepared the way for such a radical change of direction. Overcoming this handicap by the most strenuous application to his new duties, he became a leading member of the minority faction of the faculty bent on imparting new life to the stagnant curriculum rooted in the vanished outlook of the eighteenth century. But in spite of his widely applauded success as a teacher, he abandoned his academic post after a scant seven years to devote himself to the writing of history. (During his teaching years this had gradually revealed itself to him as his destined vocation.) By his prolonged submission to strict academic discipline and its attendant classroom labors he had laid up a store of scholarly energy which now drove him steadily forward on his chosen course. During the thirteen post-Harvard years, that is, between 1877 and 1890, he rose to a universally acknowledged eminence in the field on the strength of his highly original *Life of Albert Gallatin* and his unrivaled nine-volume *History of the United States of America during the Administrations of Jefferson and Madison*. A circumstance subtly expressive of Adams' expanding personality was that, on abandoning teaching for the writing of history, he exchanged the cramping academic atmosphere of Cambridge for the more animated and worldly environment of Washington. At the same time, so far as it was in him, he also discarded his parochial New England outlook to become an American in the most comprehensive meaning of the term.

In 1890 this second or historical phase ended almost as abruptly as the first or political phase. All biographical periodization has heavy drawbacks, since a life fragmentized in this manner must also, to do it justice, be seen as a continuing whole, with every new phase inescapably carrying its predecessors along with it and, with equal inevitability, foreshadowing its chronological sucessors. The relevance of this statement is sharply revealed on turning to Adams' third phase. This was marked, on the one hand, by travel and restless movement; on the other, by absorption in the natural sciences under the conviction that their mastery would disclose the all-embracing universal law of history. It must not be overlooked, however, that the natural sciences, far from being an interest of recent origin, had already begun to attract his attention while he was serving as his father's secretary at the London post. In 1894, the year in which he had been elected president of the American Historical Association, he

made the first public announcement of his scientific preoc-
cupations by means of a letter, written from abroad in lieu
of the usual address, delivered in person at the association's
annual meeting. This letter was a discussion of "The Tendency of History," and its purpose was to inform his startled
colleagues that history, regarded unanimously by them and
since its distant Greek beginnings as a department of literature, was about to lose its traditional character and become
a science.

Although occupied at that time and to the close of his life
with many interests in addition to the natural sciences, he
never again abandoned his concern with them and their al-
leged control of human history. His autobiography, *The Education of Henry Adams,* which was not published until
after his death and which has been acclaimed by more so-
phisticated Americans as his leading work, devotes its last
fourteen chapters to the exposition of the scientific theory on
which he had brooded practically all his life. And if that
does not suffice to prove his enduring preoccupation with the
problem of history as science, let us note that the last work
he personally saw through the press, his *Letter to American
Teachers of History,* assembled in elaborate detail the evidence for the oracular announcement that history was about
to become a science with which, sixteen years before, he had
shocked the members of the American Historical Association. By this closely documented *Letter* he convinced himself, though few, if any, of the hundreds of history professors
to whom he sent a copy of his argument, that he had proved
his case. The *Letter* was flavored with a pinch of diabolical
malice hard to credit in a man essentially so tenderhearted.
For the theory, if true, shattered *in toto* the high hopes en-

tertained for mankind ever since the rationalistic eighteenth century had given birth to the concept of "progress." What Adams uncompromisingly propounded in the *Letter* was, first, that history is fatefully enmeshed with the laws of force of the physical universe and, second, that this same universe is steadily, if slowly, moving toward its inescapable, ordained extinction. It follows that man, vaunted not only by the older champions of progress but also by the more recent Darwinian evolutionists as the crown of creation's millennial efforts, must travel the same downward path to annihilation. No more rigidly deterministic and starkly pessimistic future has ever been forecast for man and his world.

With the *Education* and the *Letter* we have passed beyond Adams' third stage of development into his fourth, in which, without ceasing to follow, as occasion arose, all his earlier lines of thought, he chiefly surrendered to an interest as novel as it was unexpected. The predilections of Adams' forebearers, and they in turn influenced his own, had been intellectual. They had been so exclusively intellectual that from his adolescence the sensuous world of art and nature had remained practically an unexplored continent. How this terra incognita during his third, or travel, period slowly rose into view and took complete possession of him constitutes the most fascinating of his many changes of front. The engaging process began at the close of his historical phase with two extensive journeys to the Polynesian Islands and the Orient with his artist-friend John La Farge. His letters tell, with the playful humor which is one of his epistolary charms but also with convincing assurance, how under La Farge's guidance he was awakened to the colored splendor of the Pacific island vegetation in its setting of azure seas and opal sunsets and was induced to woo an exciting intimacy with these revelations by attempting to transfer their magnificence to paper. It is impossible to doubt that his introduction to the hitherto locked world of the senses occurred in the South Seas with La Farge and that the conversion was completed when, some years later, the same traveling companion brought him face to face with the wonder of medieval glass preserved in the French cathedrals.

Overwhelmed with the glory of medieval glass, he was soon absorbed in a tranced study of medieval statuary and architecture until, coupling these expressions of the Christian faith at the highest level of its flight with the political foundations from which they made their skyward leap, he encompassed with a wholehearted devotion one of the most memorable areas of human experience. If, as his correspondence indicates, we date the start of his intense concern with the world of medieval art from 1895, during the town-to-town tour of northern France that he made with his friends, the Cabot Lodges, we may consider that date to mark the beginning of his last and crowning phase and underscore its blazing contrast with its predecessors by naming it his aesthetic phase. The noble monument he has left behind of this concluding period, the work *Mont-Saint-Michel and Chartres,* is the most penetrating book on the medieval spirit ever produced by an American.

On bringing this preliminary survey of the activities of Henry Adams to a close, the point to which it is indispensable to return is that these four phases must not be conceived as hard-and-fast compartments. Adams himself was repeatedly at pains to account for the many roads he followed by referring to himself as an outstanding example of the multiplicity of interests and directions into which the medieval unity of life and thought had been dissolved since the Renaissance and Reformation. By this confession he lends support to our procedure of breaking his life into successive periods of activity, often in acute conflict with one another. However, in spite of the fact that Adams pictured himself as illustrating the alarming mental disruption of his time and in spite of abundant material to support his view, he indisputably possessed a distinct personality which his multiple transformations tended to obscure but never succeeded in destroying. Regardless of the diverse masks he chose to wear, this personality constitutes for all readers who have ever passed under his spell his indestructible, unifying core.

There is nothing in the story of the young Henry Adams to indicate that he would ever depart from the long-established tradition of his family. He attended the proper preparatory schools at Boston and passed thence to Harvard College, where he achieved the average record of the student not overimpressed with book learning. Because of his free participation in the undergraduate social and literary activities, his classmates would seem to have held him in higher esteem than did the faculty. In evidence thereof they elected him class orator at the graduation ceremonies which took place in June, 1858. He was now twenty years old, and his resolution to proceed next to Germany to study civil, that is, Roman, law hinted a first distinct deviation from the family line; but, since he attended the opening lecture of the civil law course at Berlin and never returned, he cannot well be credited with the earnest pursuit of an educational novelty. Although lingering on in Germany and Italy for two years, he consistently refused to follow a clear-cut plan of study and, with the irresponsible zest of youth, gave himself up to the pleasant distractions of travel and desultory reading.

Not long after his return to America he re-embarked for Europe, this time to London to serve as private secretary to his father, who on Lincoln's assumption of the presidency had been appointed minister to the Court of St. James's. There can be no doubt that, in contrast to his first European trip, the young secretary was immensely stirred by the social whirl and, more particularly, by the alarming head-on collision with the pro-Confederate British government in which the American mission found itself engaged from the first day. His letters to friends as well as the articles he wrote for American newspapers during his seven-year stay give ample evidence, on the one hand, of his close study and growing mastery of the vast political complexities of Europe and, on the other hand, of the exciting new directions taken by contemporary European thought and literature. So greatly did his secretarial activities quicken his early ambition to shine as a public servant at home that, on returning to America in 1868, he settled in Washington resolved to achieve a post of political power by the only immediately available medium—the press. A sustained two-year effort ended in a disappointment so profound that it may be accepted as the starting point of that disillusionment which figured thenceforth as an unfailing feature of his thought. The possibility may not be disregarded that he had been endowed at birth with a strongly negative slant of mind, in which case the significance of the distressing Washington experience lies in its having effected the release of a tendency hitherto kept in check by what his friends noted as an ever ready, countervailing supply of youthful exuberance.

Adams has not left us in the least doubt as to the nature of the experience that rang down the curtain on his early dream of political advancement and drove him to adopt what had always teased him as a possible alternative choice, the career of literature in one or another of its many forms. We can only agree that the shift was in much happier accord with the sum of his talents than the trials imposed by officeholding under contemporary political conditions would have proved to be. However, to understand the depth of the crisis into which he was plunged by the bankruptcy of his public aspirations, it is necessary to take a backward step in time and look at the revolutionary change effected in the Boston spiritual background in the generation immediately preceding Adams' birth. Under the leadership of the top social and intellectual representatives of the city the dour Puritanism of the early settlers underwent so radical a revision that in certain essential respects the traditional religious doctrines were stood directly on their heads. Man, instead of being born totally depraved, was declared to be born without sin and to be called by God, who was no longer conceived as an avenging but as a loving deity, to live in happy harmonious fellowship with a friendly universe. Even the central trinitarian dogma of original Calvinism was abandoned in favor of a single, kindly Father, and the total movement in the light of this theological simplification announced to the world as Unitarianism.

However, the new outlook, effected in the main in the realm of reason, did not at once penetrate into the deeper seated realm of conduct. The most conspicuous manifestation of Puritanism had from its origin been the severe moral code imposed on its followers in their relations with one another. Although with the advancing empire of Unitarianism the inherited religious tenets gradually lost their hold even to the point of vanishment, the norms of social behavior long remained unaffected, thereby imposing the retention of the strict honesty and lofty probity that had for generations past ruled private and public relations alike. In other words, Unitarianism, while casting off the characteristic religious sting of Calvinism, retained its unbending ethical standards; and it was in this unchanged moral form that the generation following the advent of Unitarianism practiced the ancestral faith. This later generation was that of Henry Adams. He was an ethical, though no longer a religious, Puritan, and he confronted the devastating Washington experience with a behavior code of an as yet unimpaired severity.

The center and core of Adams' Washington experience was the head of the government, President Grant himself. Brilliant as is the portrait Adams later[1] did of Grant as a chance survival of a bygone primitive age, he does not explain any better than any other of the president's numerous portraitists how so much unashamed immorality could have clustered around Grant's person without Grant himself being the actual source of infection. And yet, hard as it is to believe, his biographers are practically unanimous in asserting his personal integrity in the face of the festering corruption of his administration. It was into this cloaca that Adams plunged headfirst, dedicating himself enthusiastically as a young journalist to the service of the new president when Grant took office in March, 1869. This president, like the first incumbent of the office, had brought a war of national scope to a triumphant close and, like his great Virginian

1. *The Education of Henry Adams* (New York: Modern Library, 1931), chap. xvii.

predecessor, would now, so Adams told himself, inaugurate a domestic policy as constructively inspired and as free from personal taint.

Only a few weeks sufficed to open the self-deceived enthusiast's eyes to a situation which, murky from the start, deepened to unrelieved blackness before Grant's first year had elapsed. The busy plunderers, who hovered around an apparently slumbering chief executive, probably never even became aware of the existence of Adams, the high-minded idealist sharply intent on their proceedings. No sooner had he taken the measure of the ruling villainy than he spurned it with fiery indignation. The sole prospect for effecting a governmental reorientation was through the organization of a vigorous and, if possible, nation-wide press campaign in behalf of reform. Fortunately Washington was full of young men as disillusioned as himself whose concerted action seemed capable of driving the harpies from the loaded tables they defiled. But the idea proved a will-o'-the-wisp, a faint glimmer that was quickly extinguished by the miasmatic vapors rising from all the departments of the administration. Defeated beyond hope of recovery, Adams despaired of corrective action within the calculable future and concluded that moral law, the sole remaining element of the ancestral religious credo, had ceased to function.[2] To complete his gloom, the lapse of ethical purpose in government impaired his faith in the closely related ancestral political heritage, the democratic system. Slowly he found himself embracing the view that political activity inescapably brings personal corruption in its train and is therefore evil in itself. Unable to

2. In the *Education* (p. 280), he summarizes his Washington defeat in the clipped phrase: "The moral law had expired."

call a halt at this turn of his reflections, he then swept on to the resolution to abandon forever the dream of publicly won laurels that had possessed him from the time when, as an eight-year-old schoolboy, he used to walk hand in hand with his venerable grandfather, former President John Quincy Adams.

In order to review soberly his loss of direction, he passed the summer of 1870 in Europe, and it was there, while on a visit to an English friend, that he received the already mentioned offer of a professorship in history at Harvard College. He did not as promptly jump at it as might be imagined. For one thing, he had scruples about accepting an office for which he had not been systematically prepared; also he was instinctively indisposed to letting himself be drawn into the academic world. The very word "professor" filled him with sharp distaste. However, no better prospect beckoned, and in the fall of 1870 he settled in Cambridge to assume the responsibilities of a college history teacher. For lack of previous training he was obliged, first of all, to teach himself, and he pursued his twofold teaching task with such exemplary fervor that he became an inspiration to his students. True, he abandoned classroom work after seven years, exchanging teaching for the writing of history, in which field he quickly achieved a reputation that put him among the masters and, after the completion in 1891 of the monumental *History of the United States of America during the Administrations of Jefferson and Madison,* at the very top.

In later life he used to speak disparagingly of the twenty-year period of his narrowly professional concern with history. It had by then become an activity he had left behind for more immediately absorbing interests. But it would be a grave mistake in the appraisal of the total man to take his disparagement at face value. For, quite apart from the *History*, which in the eyes of his fellow craftsmen takes rank as his greatest work, he acquired in those years of exacting scholarly work the habit of never giving up a quest until he had traced it backward and forward to its beginning and end. The discipline imparted by this practice left a permanent mark on his character by giving it the firmness and stability necessary to balance its excessive natural mobility.

The *History* owes its excellence to a body of authentic facts drawn by patient labor from the documents. The facts were then after scrupulous screening by a critically mature and naturally lively mind laid out as a continuing panorama of the American national development during the presidencies of Jefferson and Madison. It was a procedure combining scholarship and art, the happy union of which at their highest level has through the ages yielded a treasury of universally acknowledged historical masterworks. Foremost of these in the English language is by general consent Gibbon's *Decline and Fall of the Roman Empire.* In view of the acclaim that greeted it at its birth almost two hundred years ago and that it still elicits, we may agree that its continuing primacy remains undisputed. However, because of merits different from those of the older work but of equal importance, Adams' *History* presses it close.

Adams began this work with a cultural survey of the new republic that provided a detailed analysis of the state of civilization attained by its component sections on Jefferson's assumption of the presidency in 1801. This was a procedure which had been occasionally followed by contemporaries of Adams and pointed to an intention to enlarge

the scope of history as hitherto practiced. For since its revival in the Renaissance, history, under the direction of the
authoritative ancients, had confined itself narrowly to politics. What Adams proposed with his introductory survey was
so great an enlargement of range as to embrace a people's
total activities. These opening cultural chapters still constitute one of the most impressive features of the book. Their
welcome and necessary counterpart is offered in the *History*'s
concluding chapters, which undertake to assess the advance
in civilized living made during the sixteen years covered by
the two administrations. The present-day reader, however,
who not only accepts the broadened scope of history but
emphatically demands it as the indispensable basis of a
mature work will not fail to lament that Adams, in spite of
the happy introductory feature of his *History,* was not able
to liberate himself completely from the preponderance
traditionally conceded to political, and especially diplomatic,
material. To this critic at least, his work suffers from an excessive length resulting from a too detailed and, finally,
tedious pursuit of the minute fluctuations in the long-spun-
out diplomatic exchanges between Washington and its European antagonists. To its excessive length (nine volumes)
may be charged the regrettable fact that the *History* has
never enjoyed the broad popularity it deserves. Admirers
have therefore frequently voiced the desirability of promot-
ing its circulation by issuing an abbreviated edition. Not till
1947 was this plan carried out, when a version of the *History*
was published in two volumes under the perceptive editor-
ship of Herbert Agar.

A feature yielding the special flavor of Adams' artistry
and wit is the numerous thumbnail sketches of individuals

with which he enlivened his narrative. Each of the many actors in the historical cast appears with the particular physiognomy that made him a recognizable person in his day. Joel Barlow, for example, a man of minor importance, is presented with such sympathetic understanding enlivened with kindly humor that the close view we get of him is a pure delight. The outstanding characteristic of Barlow was an honest, but laughable, self-inflation which the ironic artistry of Adams mercilessly exposed but without reducing by a shade the respect the man otherwise deservedly inspired.

The unquestioned masterpiece of the Adams gallery is, as his public had every right to expect, the overshadowing figure of the great democrat, Thomas Jefferson. Since it was Jefferson who had buried Adams' great-grandfather, the second president and head of the Federalist party, under a landslide of popular rejection, it might be supposed that the great-grandson would let some resentment shine through his presentation of the too successful victor. But not a trace of ill-will can be discovered in the repeated portrait touches of the slayer of the Federalist dragon that vivify the text. What we are given is a balanced, clear-eyed appreciation that admirably succeeds in bringing Jefferson to life exactly as he was. An occasional sly note of humor contributes to the liveliness of the portrait by showing us the gangling, gawky frontiersman in the White House as, clad in slippers down at the heel and clothes that were too small for him and slouching on one hip with one shoulder high above the other, he held forth endlessly to a rapt group of listeners on any of a score of subjects that agitated his ever busy brain. Since the great democrat conspicuously, and in the end tragically, failed to realize any of the clamorously advertised nostrums of his pacifist program, Adams lacked no opportunity to puncture his pretensions with masterful sarcasm. But he held back, as this writer sees it, not only in order to abide by the scholarly detachment he had set as a goal for himself but also out of compassion for the presidential idealist humbled by the utter defeat of his impractical intentions.

In 1880 and again in 1884 Adams interrupted his labors on the *History* to publish two novels, titled respectively *Democracy* and *Esther*. If novels at all, they must be classified as satirical hybrids of the species brightened with occasional witty coruscations but failing to come convincingly to life because operating with character types instead of with clearly profiled individuals. The very limited interest they elicit stems from the return they mark on Adams' part to the interests he had forsworn in the wake of his crushing experience at Washington under President Grant. At that time he had broken with the political motivation of his past, never to turn back, but he could not refrain from occasionally reconsidering the settled pessimism at which he had arrived about the institutions and public morals of his country. Both novels set up a framework for discussing the possible checks on the prevailing material corruption and the parallel religious hollowness that might be countered by a reactivated ethical code and a return to the vigorous pre-Darwinian version of the Christian faith. The earlier *Democracy* considers the ethical issue, the later *Esther* weighs the possibility of an orthodox renewal. The animated discussion among the characters witnesses Adams' continuing personal concern with the state of American society but leads to no lifting of his doubts. So far as these two books go, he saw no likelihood that an attempted reform of either morals or religion would terminate the social breakup.

To these years of an all but exclusive concern with the *History* belong the absorbing episode of his marriage with Marian Hooper, a member like himself of the exalted circle of the Boston Brahmins. The marriage took place in 1872 and proved to be the happy union of two congenial spirits. Mrs. Adams was a physically delicate person of great charm and a quick wit sharpened at times to a razor's edge. Possessed, like her husband, of an independent fortune, she presided over a household, first at Cambridge and afterward on a much larger scale at Washington, which drew to it the choicest spirits of the town. Since the marriage was not blessed with children, a circumstance of great though indefinable significance, she was able to give herself freely to the many activities of social leadership that fell to her lot. But when her father, with whom she had been very close since childhood, died in 1884, her health gave way, and she plunged into an uncontrollable despondency. The devoted attentions of her husband failed to lighten her gloom, and on a December day of 1885 she committed suicide by taking poison.

The dark particular hell into which this termination of a rarely intimate companionship plunged a sensitive spirit like Adams defies description. But desolate as it left him, it did not keep him from resolutely continuing on his appointed way and winning relief from gnawing pain by resuming his labors on the uncompleted *History*. The single evidence of his continuing sorrow of which it is permitted to speak is the monument to his wife which his friend, the sculptor Augustus Saint-Gaudens, fashioned for him under his close direction. It is the famous draped bronze figure that on completion was set up in Rock Creek Cemetery at Washington and in the shadow of which her mortal remains, as, later, those of Adams himself, were consigned to earth. Human conjecture has played endlessly with the seated female form, giving it a name according to the varied response of the beholders; but none of them conveys more than fleeting satisfaction, for the figure is enveloped in the most unfathomable of all mysteries, that of life and life's twin brother death. Adams dismissed all suggested names as too confining and met its riddling inscrutability with the statement: "It asks questions, it does not answer them."

When in 1890 the *History* was at last finished Adams felt as if the Old Man of the Sea had dropped from his back and resolved to celebrate his liberation by world travel, preferably into the as yet unknown regions of Asia and the South Seas. In company with his friend the painter John La Farge he repeatedly in the course of the next few years invaded the island world of the Pacific and, as perhaps never before and certainly never afterward, dropped into an easy, carefree state of mind. Under the friendly prompting of his companion, he awoke to the color world of the tropics and even tried his hand, though admittedly with no great success, at the reproduction of its magic. The two friends settled in turn on several islands but lingered longest and most happily on Samoa. The group of letters Adams sent from this particular ocean paradise, as yet untouched by Western civilization, furnish ground for adding the gift of letter writing to his many other titles of greatness. While the letters were prompted by pure delight in an experience of legendary novelty and invest even the trivial everyday events with a sparkling freshness, they disclose also the professional historian by their depiction of the constituent elements of this primitive society and by the assigning of it to its precise place in the story of human evolution. His style had by now achieved its final form. Combining vigor with studied polish it was employed with a variety and deftness that lent it unfailing animation and distinction.

In these same years of travel he also deepened his concern with the natural sciences. His earliest interest in them dated from the furor created during his English residence by Darwin's *Origin of Species.* The natural sciences exercised a strong pull on him, not only because they excited the natural curiosity of a roaming mind, but also because they arrived or seemed to arrive at mathematically proved truths, the absence of which sorely troubled him in his chosen field of history. Why had no laws of history ever been discovered to match the universally accepted laws of science? Might it not be that the movements of nature and the stages of man's development recorded by history had been artificially isolated from each other and that the laws of the larger field of nature embraced the narrower field of man? And if that were true, did it not follow that the laws of nature were also the laws of history? He cogitated this conundrum for years till the occasion arose to make his first, but as yet tentative, communication on the subject. In 1894, in the already mentioned presidential letter to the annual meeting of the American Historical Association, he flung the cryptic message at his astonished fellow historians that their discipline, rated by them and their predecessors as a humanistic study, was about to become a science.

During the following sixteen years he failed to redeem the promise implied in his communication, but that does not mean that he forgot it. On the contrary, he worked on the problem he had posed with an intensity we would hesitate to credit did we not know the amazing vigor of his mind. Even so, one marvels at the wide range of his reading in the sciences, for he pursued at the same time a number of equally absorbing interests that culminated before he died in the two works for which he is best known by the general public, *Mont-Saint-Michel and Chartres* and the *Education of Henry Adams*. His concluding word on the identity of history and science appeared in 1910 under the title *A Letter to American Teachers of History*.

Let it be said once again that the American teachers of history completely ignored the demonstrations of their famous colleague. To this day not a single work in the field of history in America has been composed in conformity with Adams' scientific formula. Not even Adams himself followed it, for when he wrote his next and last historical work, *Mont-Saint-Michel and Chartres,* he composed it in accordance with the traditional formula of carefully gleaned facts ordered and interpreted by an individual intelligence.

While it is admitted that Adams seems to have covered in his reading the whole available literature in the natural sciences, he could only read material that had been published by the first decade of the twentieth century. He cannot, of course, be blamed for not anticipating the revolutionary discoveries in the sciences since that time, but he can and must be blamed for writing as though he believed the sciences had during his lifetime arrived at eternally unchanging truths. Since this emphatically is not the case and since science has revised and, in some instances, actually rejected the truths of Adams' day, the platform on which he rested his argument has hopelessly collapsed. This should suffice of itself to dispose of the *Letter*. Its central contention, which Adams enthroned as an absolute, was the so-called second law of thermodynamics, which affirms the dissipation or degradation of energy. Ascribing the degradation ultimately to the gradual cooling of the sun, Adams felt free to forecast the end of our earth and its creature population in ice, and he tirelessly assembled evidence from the many sister sciences of physics to prove that the movement was already, and indeed had been for some centuries past, in full swing. True, the sun's energy was so vast that it would continue to be poured forth for hundreds of millions of years, but that did not alter the eventually ordained blackout of the solar universe.

One wonders why it was that Adams marshaled all this evidence about the universally conceded consequence of the gradual failure of the sun's heat, unless it was that he found an unholy satisfaction in contemplating the end of the world for which he had lost his liking. Probably a congenital pessimist, he had certainly by his middle years developed into an outstanding specimen of that species. It is this settled negative frame of mind which, in the present writer's view, accounts for his arbitrarily and wilfully ascribing an absolute value to the second principle of thermodynamics, for by doing so he arrived at the pleasant assurance of the absolute annihilation of our unloved human kind. Since his pessimism arose out of his defeatist attitude and drove him to conclusions which not only historians but scientists as well have refused to accept, the grim Judgment Day that he saw as already threateningly suspended in the sky was dismissed as a false alarm.[3] And since its dismissal has found no objectors, save among a few similar birds of ill omen, we might spare ourselves further concern with it were it not for its effect on the later tenor of Adams' thought and life.

No reader of Adams' letters, especially of the volumes edited by Worthington C. Ford and Harold Dean Cater, can have failed to note that, as Adams attained assurance of the inevitable cosmic cataclysm, he gave up all active participation in the movements of his time. He deliberately adopted the sardonic role of a box-seat spectator at a three-ringed circus who, by reason of his unique philosophic insight, was the only one aware that the antics of the performing acrobats and clowns were nothing more than involuntary convulsions prophetic of the approaching end and who resolved to pass his time by at least getting some amusement out of them. A statement that can only shock every reader of the later letters and which occurs again and again is that the rapidly accumulating disasters at the turn of the century that led straight to the agony of World War I—the Boer War, the Dreyfus scandal, the Russo-Japanese War—afforded him the welcome "fun" of distractions from the heavy tedium of a joyless existence. As an aloof spectator of events he washed his hands of all responsibility for the breakup of civilization occurring before his eyes and refused to let it touch his heart. That, at least, was his attitude as communicated with odious frivolity to his correspondents.

3. The most recent systematic study of Adams' scientific pretensions reduces them to the shambles even unprofessional readers have long suspected them to be (see William H. Jordy, *Henry Adams: Scientific Historian* [New Haven: Yale University Press, 1952]).

But his private heartbreak over the sufferings and calamities of the world which, as a sensitive spirit, he could not escape he kept a close secret and buried in silence. Some of his letters voicing his "fun" (his constantly recurring expression) over current horrors make extremely painful reading. By taking them at face value his most bitter critic has made out that the aging Adams had become emotionally calloused and intellectually imbecile.[4]

With his *Letter to American Teachers* (together with its richly obscure Epilogue entitled "The Rule of Phase"), we have embarked on what in our introductory survey we identified as Adams' last or aesthetic phase. Obviously neither the *Letter* nor the "Phase" can be charged with having even a remote association with an aesthetic impulse. Both publications plainly stem from his long absorption in the problem of subordinating history to science by drawing it within the range of an all-embracing scientific law. That he continued the pursuit of his scientific interests in the first decade of the twentieth century, his last period of productive work, serves to confirm the assertion ventured at the outset that, in spite of his admitted mental multiplicity, he possessed an underlying unity which tied his life from boyhood to old age into a coherent whole.

Of the two remaining works of this same decade, *The Education of Henry Adams,* which is an autobiography, though with a special slant, also stems from a continuing concern with the past; but by no stretch of the imagination

4. Yvor Winters, "The Creation of Confusion" in his *The Anatomy of Nonsense* (Norfolk, Conn.: New Directions, 1943).

can an uninterrupted preoccupation with a long-meditated personal problem be avowed of its companion piece, *Mont-Saint-Michel and Chartres*. This work is convincingly the product of Adams' late conversion to an artistic outlook. In happy accord, however, with the free range of his genius the pursuit of this novel interest did not keep him from a continued attachment to such earlier inquiries as had not been brought to completion. The sufficient reason for distinguishing his closing period as his aesthetic phase is that the cult of beauty was the last accretion his personality experienced; and so glowing and at the same time so delicate was the expression it achieved in the *Mont-Saint-Michel and Chartres* that this may well, with the passing of time, rank as his leading work.

In now taking up the *Education* we shall be concerned with a work which on its publication in 1918 released a chorus of mystified and conflicting comment that has not yet died down. This vocal dissonance resulted from the plan of the book announced in the Preface that marked the peak of the baffling perversity interwoven from the beginning with the author's universally admitted genius. Let this commentator frankly reveal that the intention disclosed by Adams in the Preface strikes him as verging on a mild form of lunacy. Drawing a dubious, or rather a definitely unwarranted, conclusion from Rousseau's famous *Confessions,* it affirms that the ego has become taboo as the central concern of autobiography since the Genevan's embarrassing self-revelations. In post-Rousseauan self-disclosures it figures (and Adams in his own self-disclosure is resolved to have it figure) merely as the negligible "manikin" shaped by the effect of something that alone matters and that is called by

Adams "the toilet of education." It follows, as he expressly sets it down, that for him "the object of study is the garment, not the figure." Expanding the metaphor, he represents himself as the tailor prepared to show to students in universities and elsewhere how "to be men of the world equipped for any emergency," which he apparently regards as the objective of any truly sound educational system. As an incidental consequence "the new garment will exhibit the faults of the patchwork fitted on their fathers."

A dejected man sixty years old on undertaking the *Education,* Adams regarded himself as not a partial but a total failure and for a single reason: he had been cursed with a defective education. The core of its defect was that, elaborated in the eighteenth century, it was out of tune with the changed conditions of his lifetime. Why, in view of the great reputation he enjoyed as historian and writer, he should have been so uncompromisingly persuaded that he was a failure is something of an enigma, unless we adopt the rather widely held view that his earliest ambition was—and secretly remained—the high political office which, traditional in his family, he had abandoned as a desirable objective on encountering at close quarters the moral degradation of the Grant administration. So constantly and tiresomely does he harp on his failure and its educational cause that it is conceivable that the book would not have found many readers if, in spite of his avowal that he was eschewing what currently passed as autobiography, he had not become an autobiographer in his own despite.

The departure from plan took place in the most natural manner conceivable. To bring home the errors of his falsely inspired education, he was obliged to review his life and became so interested in the absorbing pictures he recalled of existence at Boston and Quincy and took such delight in again bringing to life the people he had met there and afterward at London and Washington that he was presently spinning one of the liveliest tales of youth and young manhood within the compass of world literature.

The fascinating story spreads over the first twenty chapters of the book and closes with his appointment at the age of thirty-three to a professorship at Harvard. It is crystal clear that the high reputation the *Education* enjoys springs from these twenty chapters, which run to about two-thirds of the volume's total text. With the twentieth chapter Adams brings his communication on himself to a close only to resume it after a lapse of twenty years with chapter xxi. Why he should have chosen to throw a cloak of silence over his middle span, which embraces his experiences between his thirty-third and his fifty-third year, remains one of the many conundrums with which the self-willed man confronted his readers throughout his work. We are left to conjecture that the years in question, which he gave first to the teaching of history and afterward to professional historical production, failed in later life to elicit his interest, and we may supplement this halting explanation with the reminder that the extremely delicate and distressing episode of his marriage also fell within this period.

With chapter xxi, entitled "Twenty Years After (1892)," Adams inaugurated the second and concluding section of the *Education* with a statement that could not be more sweepingly self-abasing: "Life was complete in 1890; the rest mattered so little!"[5] After years of travel in the South

5. P. 316.

Seas with John La Farge he had returned to the fine house that the famous architect Richardson had built for him on LaFayette Square, opposite the White House, and pictured himself as sitting there with his hands in his lap pondering how thenceforward to employ his life. In 1893 he found the answer to his uncertainties through a visit to the World's Fair at Chicago. It is necessary to recall in this connection that in terminating with chapter xx the first section of his memoirs he had once and for all rejected history, and the various philosophies on which it rested, as a worthwhile area of study. Chiefly responsible for this sharp rejection of what had thus far figured as his professional employment was his growing involvement with the natural sciences, which with their impressive and steadily growing yield of universal laws presented a striking contrast to history, the boldest generalizations of which could claim no higher authority than conjectural human opinion. The vast exhibit of power represented by the massed machines of the many divisions of the Chicago fair, manifestly a triumphant expression of the natural sciences, transmitted something of their own energy to the beholder, from which then sprouted by patient cerebration the new section of his book. Its hidden but privately avowed purpose was to draw history within the compass of the natural sciences, thereby conferring on it a validity which it had thus far sadly lacked. With this altered plan the personal reminiscences, which had made up the entrancing material of the first section, were reduced, at most, to a few scattered tidbits in the resumed work, and their rarity fully explains why the second section failed even remotely to arouse the enthusiasm that had greeted its predecessor. To put the difference between them concisely, the earlier section falls indisputably within the embrace of living literature, whereas its successor involves the cold scientific exposition of a problem which, regardless of the vigor of its treatment, was addressed not to the heart but to the mind of the reader and has the further drawback of arriving at no better than an experimental conclusion.

If we accept the shock of the Chicago fair as inaugurating the absorbed attention of Adams in the problems of science, we have in the very next year his own admission of that absorption in his startling announcement to the American Historical Association that history was about to become a science. From this preliminary acknowledgment of his deep involvement with the natural sciences he pressed onward with substantial effort until he reached the end of his quest in 1910 with his *Letter to Teachers*. As we are aware, the gist of the *Letter* was the pessimistic prediction of the ordained extinction of the world and of man. With this somber finale established to Adams' satisfaction in the *Letter,* it did not call for renewed proof in the second section of the *Education*. His interest therefore swung to the new natural energies put at man's disposal, energies such as electricity, X-ray, radium, atomic fission. While man was commonly represented as the captor of these forces, it was Adams' conviction that the truer statement was that these forces had captured man. And what did he mean by the word "force"? A force in his view was anything that did work, and the outstanding feature since the advent of the industrial age was the extraordinary multiplication of forces that were responsible for man's accelerated progress. A leading hope he entertained was accurately to chart the future of the world for at least the next fifty years; and, with this object in mind, he adopted the world's steadily increas-

ing coal output as an approximately correct measure of the
increase of available power from decade to decade. He did
not hide from himself the incalculable danger that would
arise if these vast energies were placed in the hands of frail
and irrational human beings. But in spite of his alarm he
closes the work with an unexpected attack of sentimentality
and, most unconvincingly, with the hope of a better world
by 1938, the centenary of his birth, at which time he imagined
himself returning in spirit to view the altered world situation. Since this was the eve of World War II, he would
not, if conceded his wish, have found anything to persuade
him to abandon his view of man's probable destruction
through the released, ungovernable forces of nature.

It remains to consider the *Mont-Saint-Michel and Chartres,*
which was completed in 1904 and published in 1913. We
have learned how Adams in his conversion to the aesthetic
outlook came to focus on French medieval art and, more
particularly, on the art of the twelfth century as revealed at
Mont-Saint-Michel and the art of the thirteenth century as
disclosed in the cathedral of Chartres. The writing from
the very first sentence is on so different a plane from that
of the earlier works that the reader is pushed to the conclusion that in some mysterious way Adams has changed
his nature. Abandoning the settled intellectual approach,
he concentrated at once on the feeling aroused in him by
the groined vaults, the patterned façades, the lofty spires,
the unrivaled sculptures, and the glowing glass not only of
the two churches of the title but also, with a view to broad-
ening his evidence, of other churches of that part of northern
France which was the scene of the matchless burgeoning
of medieval art.

The prevailing tone of the book is therefore subjective

and emotional but not without a liberal injection of strictly factual matter. Being, after all, a historian, Adams was led, automatically we may declare, to inquire into the origin and development not only of the edifices that had laid their particular spell on him but also into the several arts of architecture, sculpture, and painting in glass that had come to supreme expression in them. It is this critically sifted factual substructure that imparts a desirable solidity to the emotional superstructure. In his spiritually exalted mood Adams is repeatedly apologetic over his dropping to the factual commonplace; but there are few readers who will refuse to welcome it. For our Bostonian rhapsodist, however, overwhelmed by the inner harmony of the arts exhibited in the churches, the stages of their structural development together with the contemporary social changes which prompted them are of relatively small import weighed against his unshakable conviction that it was, not metaphorically but literally, the Virgin Mary who called these majestic monuments into being. Nor is the statement as romantically extravagant as at first sight it might seem to be. For every great culture has sprung from the hearts and minds of men charged with an inflamed and concentrated energy; and this energy in the case of the centuries of Adams' purview had its origin in the recent birth of an explosive enthusiasm for the merciful Mother of Jesus, whose intercession with her son was believed to temper his sharp sentence on sinners imposed by an unbending justice. The successive chapters of the book, which in artistically proportioned detail describe the towers and portals, the rose windows and apses, and the twelfth- and thirteenth-century glass, compose in their sum a canticle to Mary which, though intoned in noble prose, is enveloped in an aura of authentic poetry.

Enraptured by medieval art, Adams' never slumbering curiosity drove him into an examination of other areas of medieval activity, thereby leading him to round off his central study of cathedrals with a number of subsidiary but strictly related interests. Notable among these is his assembling of the varied evidence of the manner in which the novel worship of the Virgin mitigated the harsh traditional Christian orthodoxy; and no less notable is the view he affords of contemporary poetry and philosophy. It may be doubted that there exists anywhere in equally compact form an exposition of the cautiously skeptical philosophy of Abelard and of the unflinching orthodoxy of St. Thomas Aquinas. These additions to the main ecclesiastical matter raise the book to the level of a general survey, which it would be an exaggeration to represent as adequately covering the total period under treatment but which, within the limits it sets itself, is as loftily inspired and as lovingly tender a presentation as the English language boasts of one of the greatest ages of aspiration and achievement in the human record.

In the light of the foregoing story, the life of Henry Adams presents itself as a puzzling mixture of high achievement and ill-starred failure. The failure has become increasingly manifest since his death and turns on his attempted betrayal of the ancient and honorable department of literature called history by stripping it of its independence and depressing it to a branch of the natural sciences. While his attempt ended in universally admitted failure, it points to some flaw of mind or character about which agreement will not be easy to attain. The suggestion has been made to connect it with his pessimism, although his pessimism, at least in its final form of unbroken gloom, did not master him until after his surrender to his scientific obsession. It is more likely that his obsession induced his pessimism than the other way round. The present writer is inclined to attribute the character flaw to an excessive self-esteem such as would have been denounced as pride of intellect in the days when the world rested contentedly in the faith of a supernatural guidance. Looking backward over the monstrously disordered story of man, Adams was seized with a passion for a mathematically provable explanation of its savage confusion and ended by persuading himself he had found it by assimilating history to the natural sciences.

To provide his hypothesis with a solid substructure of fact turned out to be a labor like that of Sisyphus, for the stone he had set himself to heave uphill regularly slipped from his grasp before it reached the top and plunged once more to the bottom. Undeniably and unregrettably, he put aside his Sisyphus sorrows some years before he died, but he never expressly renounced the arrogant conviction that in the laws of the natural sciences, which, it has been proved, he never more than partially understood, he possessed the certain clue to the destiny of man. Nor was he diverted from his belief by the fact that the destiny he forecast for man deprived him of every influence on the course of his own development by reducing him to a helpless victim of the blind, unaccountable powers of nature.

However, in spite of Adams' dedication of a large portion of his life to an unprofitable scientific concept, he was born and essentially remained throughout his days a devoted humanist. Basically considered, that meant he was endowed at birth with lively senses and a penetrating intelligence that enabled him to face the facts of life and history with an undaunted vigor, freshness, and delight. It is to this endowment conferred on him as a free gift by the gods that he owed the production of certain works which won him fame in his lifetime and for which he will continue to be honored as long as American literature survives. They are not so numerous as they might have been had he not been diverted by his colossal scientific aberration. While they include that portion of his letters (and it is by far the larger portion) not darkened by his ever deepening pessimism, they embrace as their outstanding titles his *History of the United States of America during the Administrations of Jefferson and Madison,* the frankly biographical sections of *The Education of Henry Adams,* and the incomparable disclosure of the Middle Ages at the point of their loftiest reach revealed in his *Mont-Saint-Michel and Chartres.* On the strength of his abiding works he must therefore be rated as essentially a humanist. But that is not the last word of the praise that is his due. By virtue of a command of style and form as native to him as his swift mind and vivid senses, he became that rare variety of humanist who by reason of his finished artistry assumes a place among the immortal historians.

BIBLIOGRAPHICAL NOTE

It is only the most eminent of Adams' works that are treated in this essay. They are *The History of the United States of America during the Administrations of Jefferson and Madison, The*

Education of Henry Adams, Mont-Saint-Michel and Chartres, The Tendency of History, A Letter to American Teachers of History. Attention has also been given to his letters, particularly to the collection in two volumes edited by Worthington C. Ford and to the collection compiled by Harold Dean Cater under the title *Henry Adams and His Friends*.

Among the many essays and books dealing with Henry Adams the reader is referred to *Runaway Star: An Appreciation of Henry Adams* by Robert A. Hume (Ithaca, N.Y.: Cornell University Press, 1951) first for its own sake but also for its apparently complete Bibliography.

NOTES ON HISTORIOGRAPHY[1]

I. ACHIEVEMENTS OF THE GREEKS

What a debt our present civilization owes to the Greeks! In politics the democratic idea is embodied in the free city-state; in architecture the simplicity and harmony of the temple; in sculpture idealized projections of living form; in drama works of art which illuminate the ways of God with man; and in philosophy, which includes science, they declared for the acquisition of knowledge in order that men might become better masters of their destiny.

Is it possible to reduce these achievements to a common denominator, to pack the work of the Greeks into a single sentence? I think it is: the Greeks brought intelligence or reason into play as no people before them. Instead of cringing before the powers of nature, man was to use his intelligence to improve his position. They were the first people to take that position, and every people to take it since is walking in their footsteps.

It is this intelligence that gave birth to history. What is history? It is a branch of literature—that branch which deals with the

1. A marginal comment by Ferdinand Schevill, dated June 21, 1952, states that these notes, selections from which I have edited, were drawn up as a guide for a lecture course he gave at the University of Puerto Rico from January through March, 1945. Unfortunately some of the notes are missing. I have included these selections because they reflect his views on several famous historians, some of whom he intended at one time to include in this book. There is also additional material about his views on the nature of history. The first part of these notes dealing with the Greeks dates back to history lectures which he gave at the University of Chicago in 1932 and 1933. It must be remembered that when lecturing he filled out these notes with supplementary comments from his broad and varied background.—JAMES SCHEVILL.

recovery of past events and their orderly presentation. There are always two parts: (1) research, (2) composition.

Homer and Myth

In the *Iliad* and the *Odyssey* Homer incidentally tells us a good deal about the ideas of the ancient Greeks, their social habits, and their political institutions. But the events these epic poems record are not history; they are inventions of the old bards or poets—they are myths. Myths always precede history. Myths arise when an actual event is armed with fabulous elements, with new statements added by each new poet until the original event has been transformed and is completely buried under layers of invented stuff.

Thus for centuries myth ruled, and there was no history. Then around 600 B.C. came the great mental revolution of which Thales of Miletus was the first product. Greek life and thought expanded. Still, for a long time, there was no interest in the orderly presentation of past events. An occasional single event was recorded. Men became interested in their descent and constructed genealogies. These genealogies in their ascension usually ended in a god. Great men were pleased to imagine that they came from a god. These early genealogies were, nonetheless, a step toward history.

Appearance of Herodotus

In the fifth century the time was ripe and Herodotus appeared. He was born in 484 B.C. at Halicarnassus in southwestern Asia Minor and died in 425 B.C. We know very little about him and what we know we get from his book. He traveled extensively over the then known world. Internal evidence shows that he was in Egypt, Syria, Babylonia, Persia, and in every section of Greece and southern Italy. Why did he travel? It is at least reasonable to suppose that he traveled to collect data for his history. What other way was there? A modern historian need not leave the vicinity of a first-rate library to find histories and printed sources. Herodotus had no previous histories to read, no archives, no libraries. He had to interview men and take down their statements. And he says so: "I will write the history of the wars between the Greeks and Persians on the basis of an inquiry [*historia*]."

He sets about his task in a rambling fashion. It was in western Asia Minor that the Greeks came in contact with the Persians, so he speaks of the Persian penetration and presently is moved to tell the story of the Persian Empire. But Persia conquers Egypt, and so he tells the story of Egypt; Persia conquers Babylonia, and he tells that story. In short the work becomes a history of the Near East with all its peoples and customs. At last he gets back to the Greco-Persian conflict (to Marathon and Salamis), but death overtook him before he could get further with his history than the year 479 B.C.

How does this first history rate? It is a notable research deserving its high fame. But some modern critics have pointed out weaknesses. (1) They charge Herodotus with digressions due to his love of a good story. This charge is true: some of his stories are good, others wearisome. Herodotus is garrulous and anecdotal, but that does not keep his book from having an essential unity. It is always about the struggles of Greeks and Persians. (2) They charge Herodotus with credulity and inaccuracy. This charge is also true. He set down what he heard. But he applied the norm of reason. The Athenians say this, the Spartans say that. He made gross errors (e.g., about Egyptian history), but that was not his fault; it was the fault of his Egyptian informants. (3) They charge him with being a conservative. Again, this charge is true. Herodotus was affected by the new and critical views of the gods. But he did not become an unbeliever. Herodotus' conservatism shows most in his respect for the oracle of Apollo at Delphi. He believed, like Aeschylus and Sophocles, that the gods ruled and that their justice prevailed. But history is not a record of what the gods did, but what men do. History is a human record. Men make their own decisions and have to suffer the consequences of their acts. History moves on a human plane.

II. TWO ROMAN HISTORIANS

Livy (59 B.C.–A.D. 17)

Livy was a patriotic Roman who believed the gods favored his people because they followed the gods and led earnest moral lives. He has a high moral tone but no more sense of social change than other ancients. He used many sources and mentions them. But as the sources have vanished, it is impossible to say how critical he was. Scholarship was not his main interest; this keeps him from being dull. Only about one-third of the 140 books of his history have reached us. His rhetorical device of speeches becomes very tiresome to us. His history is full of signs and wonders. The miracles that happen are due to the intervention of the gods. Livy was a pious man and a good patriot.

When it comes to the old legends (that Rome was founded by Aeneas, the refounding of Rome by Romulus and Remus, etc.), Livy is frankly skeptical. He had a fund of common sense and the legends ran counter to that possession. He used all the available written sources, e.g., the tablets of Fabius Pictor on the second Punic War. We cannot tell how well he used them.

His style is vivacious and highly readable. There is a zest about the old Roman that transferred itself to his writings, especially to his writings about campaigns. He is not a rhetorician but uses the rhetorical device of speeches.

Cornelius Tacitus (A.D. 55–120)

Tacitus was a man of senatorial rank who held high office under the Flavian emperors (Vespasian, Titus, Domitian) and under Trajan. He had the customary aristocratic prejudice. He hated the emperors as usurpers but hated them more when they were tyrants. He was a man of dour, severe temper, a kind of puritan who grieved over the public corruption of his day and the spread of private immorality. Like every other author, he walks through his books: a man of high authority and dignity with a frown on his face, for he is out of tune with public and private life.

He speaks of his sources over and over again as "the writings of former times," but he is not specific. We can say that he wanted to get at the truth, but, as in the case of all the ancients, the material was insufficient by our standards. A flaw in the work of Tacitus from our modern viewpoint is that we demand a picture of social change. For us the historical process is central. Tacitus enumerates great events, and this makes a broken story in the nature of annals. His strength is portraiture, for Tacitus is a great artist. His portrait of Tiberius is one of the best-known of all history: the most sinister man who ever walked the stage of life. However, modern historians have reviewed the source material and arrived at a different opinion. There is evidence of a monumental prejudice on the part of Tacitus. But the persistence of his portrait bears witness to his powers.

III. THE RATIONALIST HISTORIAN

Although there are examples of rationalist history writing in every European country, Voltaire, the Frenchman, and Gibbon, the Englishman, are about the only ones that have survived. What do we mean by a rationalist historian? He belongs, in the main, to the eighteenth century and has cast off the leading prejudices of the immediate past, above all religious prejudices. He wishes to avoid emotion and to govern himself by the cool norm of reason.

Voltaire had hardly died and Gibbon was still alive when the French Revolution occurred. It was a product of many forces, rationalism being one. In the eyes of the intelligentsia, rationalism was the leading force. When the convulsion of the French Revolution was over, another mental atmosphere ruled—romanticism. The result was romantic history.

Edward Gibbon (1737–94)

Not only in England but throughout Europe there was immediate appreciation of Gibbon's *Decline and Fall of the Roman Empire,* and it was hailed as a masterpiece. It is still so regarded. Many hold it to be the only work worthy of being associated with the greatest classical authors on account of the dignity of style and the weight of its contents. Its form is indeed classical and its contents as impressive as its form—even more so. Gibbon had an advantage over the ancient historians by reason of the abundance of printed books and published sources. The age of erudition had preceded him. Therefore Gibbon's facts stand to this day. He is weakest in Byzantine history because little preliminary work had been done in this field. His style is of unapproachable majesty. He commanded every resource of the literary artist—balanced sentences, epigrammatic statement, irony, sarcasm, etc.

The most famous section of the *Decline and Fall* deals with the origins of Christianity. This earned him the title of heretic; extremists held him to be a satanic writer, an atheist. The heat has gone out of this controversy. There is no note of mockery in the general agreement that he wrote as a rationalist and not as a Voltairian. This means he did not regard Christianity as divinely established. It was a purely human development—a view that offended both Catholics and Protestants. Up to the time of Gibbon, only Christian evidence was taken into account (stories of persecutions, martyrs, and miracles). Gibbon weighed the evidence of pagan writers and got a more moderate story.

To this day if you believe that Christianity was divinely established, you will object to Gibbon. But if you believe it was a transformation of human society to be re-created from all available evidence, I do not see how you can cancel out Gibbon's story. Not only in his treatment of Christianity but in another respect he differs from Voltaire. Voltaire pointed to a new type of history that took in, besides politics, social classes, economic conditions, manners, laws, philosophy, and art. There is not much of this in Gibbon. He was content to treat of the state, its rulers, and its fortunes. His subject matter is chiefly wars and the administration of public affairs.

IV. THE ROMANTIC HISTORIAN

The romantic historian comes after the French Revolution and registers a conscious reaction to the rationalist viewpoint. He rejects reason in favor of an emotional approach. This may take many forms. The commonest is patriotism, a passionate love of country. As the French Revolution was anti-religious and anti-monarchical, the romantics exalted religion and monarchy and the Middle Ages. You can put it this way: the romantic historian has a thesis and distorts his facts in its favor. But it cannot be denied that the romantic historians grubbed for the facts. They were devoted to documents, but they read them in their own manner. This should warn us in the important matter of documents. Many people hold that if a historian employs documents, he is safe. Not at all; you cannot investigate how he uses the documents.

Jules Michelet (1798–1874)

Michelet was a historian who felt the need to "resurrect" the past. To do this required research, intelligence, and emotional participation. Of his *History of France* he published the first volume in 1833 and by 1843 had brought the work to the close of the Middle Ages. There is no anti-clericalism here. The change begins in 1843 when he entered the struggle against the Jesuits, who threatened to take over the French educational system. He became an impassioned partisan. From now on the Catholic church was the enemy (as with Voltaire). He revised his opinions of the Middle Ages ("a thousand years during which humanity made no progress"). What does he mean by progress? Liberty!

His *History of France* covers seventeen volumes and was finished in 1867. The first part ranks higher than the postmedieval period. His *History of the French Revolution* is a separate work written between 1843 and 1855. Only after 1855 did he resume his *History of France*. He wrote like a contemporary revolutionist. If you want dead men, dead events, brought to life, here they are! Brought to life as friends or enemies, pictured with sympathy or loathing. The story is that of liberty; there are only subjective values. If this is what you like, this is what you like. But it does not mean that you like history. You like life, excitement, entertainment, the philosophy of freedom.

Did he use the "sources"? Yes, he did. But since he distorted them to make them yield his message, the use of sources loses its meaning. Michelet is the perfect romantic.

Thomas Carlyle (1795–1881)

A Calvinist of Scotch origin, Carlyle got free of his religion, but never of his moralism. He never ceased believing in the curse of Adam. Men were fundamentally evil and needed the leadership of great men. Hence his hero-worship. Although he did not share the usual romantic beliefs—liberty, the Middle Ages, nationalism —his outlook made him a romantic in reverse, a pessimist. There is nothing in his main works (*French Revolution, Letters and Speeches of Oliver Cromwell, Life of Frederick the Great*) of what we would call the "historico-social process," and there is little enough of the traditional presentation of politics. He makes no attempt to analyze the forces that shape society. Most professional historians make light of him. There are common people in his *French Revolution* moved by revolutionary ideas, and there are leaders and would-be leaders. The real leaders he pictures are Mirabeau and Danton. The would-be leaders are Lafayette and

Robespierre. They are all pictured with extraordinary vividness. Carlyle has a kind of Cyclopean style, the opposite of Macaulay's smooth prose. But the individuals he portraitizes, the scenes he paints on canvases as large as church walls, have a color and force that have never been excelled. Although he is scorned by most professional historians (e.g., by Barnes), like Michelet, he is read eagerly, especially by the young.

V. HISTORY IN THE NINETEENTH AND
TWENTIETH CENTURIES

There were many reasons for the extraordinary expansion of history during the nineteenth century. The chief one was the multiplication of collections of documents of which the *Monumenta Germaniae historica* is the leading example. Documents were discovered in the fields of legal history, institutional history, economic history, which made possible novel histories of these subjects. New fields of study like anthropology and ethnology came into being. The study of the distant past gave us archeological studies like Egyptology and Assyriology. The study of distant continents for the first time revealed China, Japan, India. The history of literature and the history of art received increasing attention. In short, Western man became history-minded.

But that meant a revolution in viewpoint. It meant that man was no longer content to study objects as they were, but he wanted to know how they became what they were. Man recognizes the process of change and that change is continuous. This new insight culminated in 1859 in Darwin's *Origin of the Species* (the doctrine of evolution). It took billions and billions of years to give us the earth as we have it. Millions for the vegetable covering and other millions for its animal forms. No wonder the historian was greatly disturbed. He had, in the main, for hundreds of years written political history. But now there were all these other fields of history. A great variety of practice followed: some historians sticking conservatively to political history; others adding something of the new riches. When you pick up a history published after 1875 and, especially, after 1900, you can never be sure beforehand how it will define history—what its inclusions will be.

Let us concede this prevailing confusion. This has led to attempts at synthesis by which the diverse tendencies might be brought together into a new unity. Such attempts are called the "philosophy of history"—the history of man reduced to its essence. In most of these philosophies, the essence was found in the concept of "progress," a rationalist concept of the eighteenth century based on the amazing advances due to science and industry. The end might be perfection (Turgot, Holbach, Condorcet). The reaction after 1815 obscured this concept of progress. The romantics took over the concept, but they ascribed it to God. Herder, who died in 1803, wrote the most famous of these romantic philosophies. Herder, too, accepts progress as the master theme of man's history. But he refers progress to God. God has created man on a low, savage level, but God also gives him strength to raise himself to a higher level. Man has the possibility of increasing his intelligence, his command of nature, his ethical sense. The goal of endeavor is freedom, and, according to Herder's scheme, man is approaching the realization of this ideal.

The trouble with Herder and other Germans and Europeans of this school is that their philosophy lacks historical content. It is metaphysics and of the stuff of dreams. So much for progress as a unifying theme.

Another attack on the dispersion of history is the acceptance of a new type of history, the history of civilization. Here, the unit of study is not political history but the total culture. The greatest creation of man is not government but civilization, as in Oswald Spengler's *Decline of the West.* This work is opposed to the progress concept. It is based on the concept of a historical cycle. Every civilization is born, develops, dies. He tried to prove his theory by the Greco-Roman civilization and prophesied that it would fit our own. In recent times Arnold Toynbee in *A Study of History* has made an even more ambitious attempt in the same field.

An entirely different attack on history originated with Auguste Comte, who died in 1857. Overwhelmed by the success of the natural sciences, Comte thought they gave "positive" results and that the laws they developed would remain eternally valid. He declared that the time had come to apply the method of the natural sciences to man and to express the past, present, and future in terms of law. By this procedure history, as practiced in the past, would disappear to be replaced by sociology. The movement, because it replaced uncertainty by certainty, was called Positivism.

Comte invented the word sociology and may be regarded as the father of the specialties gathered under that name. Comte is a great figure, but he erred in one respect. He said history would be swallowed up by sociology and that there would be no more history. History is still as lively an interest as ever. Comte based his theory on a logical misconception. History is concerned with organized society, and organized society has from the first given birth to a steady succession of unique events. History has the task of describing these events and connecting them causally. It tells a continuous tale which excites human interest and will never cease to excite human interest. Therefore history persists. But sociology came to birth at its side. This field studies social activities—production, distribution, sanitation, hospitalization, education, population—to come to conclusions helpful to their improvement. Sociology exists side by side with history, and neither encroaches on the other.

Conclusion.—History still, in the main, is what it has been since Herodotus invented the form. The major changes are (*a*) the recent expansion of subject matter and (*b*) the recent severity of scholarly method. This has misled many to call it a science. You may, if you will, call its method scientific, but the finished product belongs to the world of art.

PRINTED IN U.S.A.